THEATRE SYMPOSIUM

A PUBLICATION OF THE SOUTHEASTERN THEATRE CONFERENCE

Elizabethan Performance

in North American Spaces

Volume 12

D0109331

Published by the

Southeastern Theatre Conference and

The University of Alabama Press

THEATRE SYMPOSIUM is published annually by the Southeastern Theatre Conference, Inc. (SETC), and by The University of Alabama Press. SETC nonstudent members receive the journal as a part of their membership under rules determined by SETC. For information on membership write to SETC, P.O. Box 9868, Greensboro, NC 27429-0868. All other inquiries regarding subscriptions, circulation, purchase of individual copies, and requests to reprint materials should be addressed to The University of Alabama Press, Box 870380, Tuscaloosa, AL 35487-0380.

THEATRE SYMPOSIUM publishes works of scholarship resulting from a single-topic meeting held on a southeastern university campus each spring. A call for papers to be presented at that meeting is widely publicized each autumn for the following spring. Authors are therefore not encouraged to send unsolicited manuscripts directly to the editor. Information about the next symposium is available from the editor, Susan Kattwinkel, Theatre Department, College of Charleston, 66 George St., Charleston, SC 29424; (843) 953-8218; kattwinkels@cofc.edu.

THEATRE SYMPOSIUM
A PUBLICATION OF THE SOUTHEASTERN THEATRE CONFERENCE

Volume 12   *Contents*   2004

Introduction

THE ESSAYS IN THIS volume were selected from the papers presented at the March 2003 SETC Theatre Symposium, "Elizabethan Performance in North American Spaces." The conference was held at Mary Baldwin College, with support from that school's administration and faculty. What made Mary Baldwin such a terrific site for the conference was the campus interest afforded by its master of letters and MFA in Shakespeare and Renaissance Literature in Performance programs and the presence and cooperation of Shenandoah Shakespeare, a professional theatre company based at Blackfriars Playhouse, a reconstruction of London's sixteenth-century private theatre. During the course of the weekend, besides engaging in inspired discussion revolving around the presented papers, we were able to tour the Blackfriars Playhouse, with Shenandoah Shakespeare's executive director, Ralph Cohen, as our guide, and view a fascinating production in that theatre of Francis Beaumont's *Knight of the Burning Pestle*.

Presentations focused on the uses and development of various North American spaces for the production of Elizabethan, primarily Shakespearean, works. The language we used was strongly influenced by the keynote talks presented by Franklin J. Hildy and Vanessa Schormann, both of whom discussed reconstructions of Elizabethan performance spaces created in North America and elsewhere in the twentieth century, as well as the challenges posed to those using such spaces. Discussions of the physical space informed those of language, style, costume, and design, as well as historical styles of production and the current "original practices" approach to Elizabethan production.

Discussions during the weekend covered historical topics from the

Elizabethan Revival to postmodernism, performance genres from popular theatre to solo performance to original practices, more than two hundred years of theatrical history, and performance spaces from reconstructed Elizabethan theatres to found space. Despite the wide variety of topics, however, the same concepts arose again and again: authenticity, minimalism of design, audience behavior and reaction, legitimizing factors of reconstruction and performance, and issues surrounding the variety of approaches to the production of Elizabethan theatre in North America. Drs. Hildy and Schormann responded to these ideas in the symposium discussion at the end of the weekend, the transcript of which (including their more recent thoughts) appears here.

The articles published in this issue offer a glimpse into that wide variety of topics covered during the weekend of the symposium and also illustrate the common concepts that connected all the talks. The first articles cover various aspects of "original practices" movements and examine various ways that scholars and critics have reinterpreted history to fit their own creative or intellectual needs. Richard Palmer traces the history of the first of those movements, the Elizabethan Revival, in the United States, particularly the work of Ben Greet. Aaron Anderson also looks at the history of revival movements but focuses on fight choreography, specifically examining the historical body and audience response. David Carlyon rounds out the pre-twentieth-century topics with his look at the "Shakespearean" work of Mark Twain and Dan Rice and the misinterpretations of contemporary scholars and critics. Kevin Wetmore also looks at a category of popular performance but a more recent one. He examines how rock-and-roll music and contemporary Shakespearean production legitimize one another in contemporary practice. Another foray into postmodern performance style is explored by Sarah Ferguson and Annie Smith. They analyze authenticity and adaptation issues presented by the production of *The Falstaff Project* produced at the University of British Columbia, Frederic Wood Theatre.

The rest of the articles examine specific reconstructions from practical and theoretical points of view. Susan Cole and Richard Hay detail the performance space at the Oregon Shakespeare Festival, looking at its design and performance history as part of a continuum of such spaces in North America. Johanna Schmitz considers issues of authenticity and location in reconstructions of Elizabethan theatres. The keynote papers of Franklin J. Hildy and Vanessa Schormann continue those considerations. Hildy explores what some reconstructions have taught us about historical production methods and audiences and speculates on what information they might teach us about our own productions and audiences. Schormann looks at the reasons for such reconstructions and the impact they have had on production. The volume concludes with an excerpt from the transcript of the closing discussion by Drs. Hildy and Schormann.

I would like to thank my immediate predecessor, Noreen Barnes-McLain, for her guidance and support, and previous editors John Frick, Phil Hill, and Tom Stephens for their continuing assistance and willingness to respond to my requests for editing help. Betsey Baun and the SETC office take care of the logistical matters of the journal throughout the year. My associate editor, Scott Phillips, greatly assisted in the editing work for this volume; his thoroughness and expertise were invaluable. Virginia Francisco and Michelle Bassett were excellent conference hosts and organizers at Mary Baldwin College, and my own department at the College of Charleston provided the time and resources I needed to complete this volume.

SUSAN KATTWINKEL
COLLEGE OF CHARLESTON

America Goes Bare

Ben Greet and the Elizabethan Revival

Richard H. Palmer

Esther Dunn, in her popular press *Shakespeare in America,* published in 1939, could write, "We know now and act upon the knowledge that Shakespeare's plays were produced with a minimum of scenery and stage illusion."[1] How did we come in America to "act upon" this knowledge that challenged a tradition of scenically spectacular Shakespeare dating from the English Restoration?

Except for amateur experiments in England by William Poel and in America by George Pierce Baker, the reconceptualization of Shakespeare's staging in the "Elizabethan mode" was largely a scholarly exercise in article writing during the decades around the beginning of the twentieth century. The application of these ideas to the professional theatre and their dissemination to an emerging college theatre coterie fell to a British actor-manager, Philip Ben Greet, in a series of Broadway and college productions in America between 1903 and 1914.

Early revivals of Elizabethan staging are widely associated with William Poel. His 1881 production of the First Quarto *Hamlet* in St. George's Hall, London, although not followed by other fully staged productions for over a decade, set a largely unchanged pattern for his work. His setting, designed to convert halls or proscenium-arch theatres into a semblance of an Elizabethan stage, had features recognizable in most subsequent reconstructions, including that of Sam Wanamaker's New Globe in London: a deep forestage intersected by two columns supporting the "heavens," a balcony, "an inner below," and two tiers of galleries at the stage ends. The one idiosyncrasy that persisted in Poel's staging, but was subsequently discredited, was the use of a traveling curtain across the onstage pillars, which enabled him to retain the deep stage / shallow stage conventions of the proscenium-arch theatre, although in this case entrances could be made from the ends as well as the middle of the curtain.

After several years of work as an actor and stage manager in various venues, Poel returned to Shakespeare in 1887, directing a series of readings for the Shakespeare Reading Society. Here he developed a more rapid delivery of the text without pauses for act or scene breaks. The absence of scenery was as much the result of these being readings as it was of any particular rejection of Victorian scenic conventions. From 1891 on, some of these presentations put readers in Elizabethan costume; so the transition back to fully staged productions was a gradual one. In 1893 Poel presented three performances of *Measure for Measure* with a stage setting designed to replicate the Elizabethan Fortune Theatre within the proscenium of the Royalty Theatre. Poel did his best to convert the Royalty Theatre, building an apron stage that thrust several feet into the auditorium, picking up the decorations of the Royalty's proscenium arch for the onstage Fortune Theatre boxes, and placing an Elizabethan facing on the first set of Royalty boxes.[2] Where Poel, in the 1881 *Hamlet* and in most of his subsequent productions, used painted drapes to cover the wings with a replication of the Elizabethan galleries, at the Royalty he built onstage galleries to match the redecorated house boxes and created seating for "onstage" spectators dressed in Elizabethan costume.

The reviewer C. E. Montague, writing at that time for the *Manchester Guardian*, astutely placed Poel's work in the context of Victorian antiquarianism:

> Mr. Poel did wonders, but he could not get rid of the proscenium arch. What he gave us was not an Elizabethan stage as it was to Elizabethan playgoers, but a picture of an Elizabethan stage seen through the frame of a modern proscenium. So we gained a good visual idea of a Shakespearean stage, but not the Elizabethan sensation of having an actor come forward to the edge of the platform in the midst of ourselves.[3]

Poel, much as Ludwig Tieck had done with his 1842 production of *A Midsummer Night's Dream* in Dresden, used the Elizabethan theatre as a scenic background for a proscenium-arch production with antiquarian ambitions.

As a result of this production of *Measure for Measure*, Poel, in 1894, formed the Elizabethan Stage Society, which, over eleven years, presented thirty productions, including eight of Shakespeare's plays, until it was dissolved in 1905 because of financial difficulties. Only four of these productions were in theatres; the others were presented in courtyards or large halls, in some cases transformed by Poel's painted curtains, in others presented before the surviving or reconstructed decorative screens that were common architectural features at one end of Elizabethan halls.

After the demise of the Elizabethan Stage Society Poel continued to produce Elizabethan plays, for a few performances each, in halls or minor theatres, continuing to advocate the staging principles he had developed in the nineteenth century. Although he converted a number of important directors and managers to the idea of platform staging before his death in 1934, Poel did little to bring about a timely change in commercial productions of Shakespeare. Herbert Beerbohm Tree and Johnston Forbes-Robertson, among others, dominated West End Shakespeare, continuing Henry Irving's tradition of highly scenic, "illusionist" productions.[4] The rebuilding of the Festival Theatre at Stratford-upon-Avon in 1932 as a picture-frame stage, an albatross with which the Royal Shakespeare Festival still struggles, indicates the thorough entrenchment of scenic Shakespeare. The mainstream of Shakespeare production remained untouched by Poel's crusade.

In America Harvard's George Pierce Baker, as with so many other things theatrical, was a principal innovator with Elizabethan staging. Baker may have participated in a bare-stage production of *Julius Caesar* in 1885 at the Sanders Theatre, the proscenium-arch theatre used by Harvard for both student and visiting productions.[5] In 1895 Baker heard that students at the Empire Dramatic School, under the direction of Franklin Sargent, were reviving Ben Jonson's *Epicoene*, and he arranged for the Sanders to be decorated as an imitation of the Fortune Theatre, much in the same manner as Poel had at the Royalty a year earlier.[6] Baker's biographer, Wisner Payne Kinne, claims that Baker had no knowledge of Poel's experiments,[7] but this seems a bit improbable given Baker's immersion in the scholarship of the English theatre. Nonetheless, Baker's reconstruction more closely resembled the Swan drawing of Johannes de Witt, rediscovered in 1888, than it did Poel's drapery-laden reconstruction.

Baker seems to have abandoned his replica setting to the Delta Upsilon fraternity, whose students staged a series of annual Elizabethan revivals, but in 1904 Baker invited the British actor Johnston Forbes-Robertson to perform *Hamlet* with a student cast under Baker's direction on another Elizabethan stage replica, this one more closely resembling the work of Poel, whose *Henry V* production Baker had seen during a 1901–2 visit to England. Like Poel, Baker advocated Cecil Brodmeir's idea that a traverse curtain between the onstage pillars divided the Shakespearean stage into zones that allowed upstage tableaux in the Victorian manner.[8]

Baker's interest in Elizabethan staging culminated in his 1907 book *The Development of Shakespeare as a Dramatist*, the best assemblage up to that time of documents relating to the Elizabethan theatre, but Baker's interests, thankfully for the American theatre, turned thereafter to other matters, such as the development of new playwrights, theatre education, and, perhaps more incidentally, the outdoor historical pageant. Significantly, when Baker had another opportunity to direct a Shakespearean play, *The Winter's Tale* at Yale in 1931, he used a Donald Oenslager New Stagecraft drape-and-platform setting tucked happily behind the proscenium, without a balcony in sight. Philip Ben Greet ties all of this disparate activity together. He officially transmitted Poel's ideas to America, performed under Baker's sponsorship, and did more than anyone else to expose Americans to minimalist staging of Shakespeare. Greet was instrumental in introducing Poel's mode of staging to the Festival Theatre at Stratford-upon-Avon, for establishing the Old Vic as a major twentieth-century producer of Shakespeare, and for cofounding the outdoor theatre in London's Regent Park, which still does summer productions of Shakespeare's plays. He was knighted in 1929, seven years before his death, largely in recognition of his role in touring productions of Shakespeare for London schoolchildren.

Performing without scenery was less a matter of principle for Ben Greet than a correlative of performing out of doors in a natural setting or in found spaces with a low-budget touring company. Greet was quick to make a virtue of necessity and espouse the cause of bare staging when it seemed academically fashionable to do so, but when means were at his disposal, he quickly reverted to scenic spectacle. As Cary Mazer states in *Shakespeare Refashioned*, his 1981 study of Elizabethan plays on Edwardian stages, primarily in Britain, "Greet was not, by disposition, an Elizabethanist."[9]

Greet had begun touring with outdoor performances of Shakespeare in England in 1886. Known variously as the Ben Greet Players, Woodland Players, or Pastoral Players, his company of young actors performed in the summer months in college gardens, the parks of Great Houses, or village greens. Among the young actors who received early training in his companies were Harley Granville Barker, Mrs. Patrick Campbell, Lilah McCarthy, C. Rann Kennedy, Edith Wynne Matthison, Constance Crawley, Sybil Thorndike, Sydney Greenstreet, and Leslie French.

During winter months Greet produced a mixture of musical comedies, Shakespeare, and popular dramas, largely in provincial theatres with occasional appearances in small London theatres. All of these indoor productions, including those of Shakespeare's plays, used the expected scenery. For instance, the highlight of the 1894/95 national tour of the Ben Greet Players was an invitation to the Stratford Festival Theatre for the Shakespeare Birthday celebration. In the course of six days they presented eight performances of a mixed repertory, including four Shakespeare plays. All were presented with the most sumptuous pictorial staging that Greet could muster.[10] The Stratford performances did not include *A Midsummer Night's Dream*, which the company later presented, advertised "with new scenery built by J. T. Bull of London and H. G. Pidgeon of Oldham,"[11] an indication of Greet's continuing focus on scenic Shakespeare.

Greet had seen a production of the Elizabethan Stage Society as early as 1895. Robert Speaight, Poel's biographer, records that Greet was so impressed with Lilah McCarthy's performance in Poel's *Twelfth Night* that he hired her for his tours.[12] When Greet's company returned to the Stratford Theatre in October of 1901 with single performances of two modern plays, Greet also sponsored an afternoon matinee of Poel's production of *Henry V*, which had been performed four days earlier at Oxford with the same cast. In this instance Poel must have abandoned his usual practice of using amateur actors because Edith Wynne Matthison, who was a regular with Greet, played the chorus in *Henry V*, and Greet's company gave subsequent performances in Peterborough, Rugby, and Camberwell.

On three successive Saturdays in the summer of 1901 Poel had staged the medieval play *Everyman* in the Master's Court of the Charterhouse at Westminster Abbey. The production was repeated in a quadrangle at Oxford in August and the following May, of 1902, moved inside to St. George's Hall. The latter production was coproduced by Ben Greet and seems to have used a setting with a raised pavilion for God and a back wall with several Gothic-arched doorways.[13] Greet's production, with Edith Wynne Matthison playing Everyman, ran for a month at the Imperial Theatre in London and then toured a number of cities, including Dublin and Edinburgh.[14] Greet was also listed as codirector with Poel of an Elizabethan Stage Society production of Ben Jonson's *The Alchemist*, presented at the Imperial Theatre for two performances in July of 1902, but with only a few changes the cast was largely the same as Poel's 1899 production of the same play. *Everyman* was the only production of the Elizabethan Stage Society to make money, and Poel sold the American production rights for £500 plus royalties to that most commercial of producers, Charles Frohman, who in turn engaged Ben Greet to organize an American tour for the 1902–3 season.

Greet presented the play at Mendelssohn Hall in New York in October of 1902, precipitating a number of positive reviews, including a lengthy paean by John Corbin, the *New York Times* critic, who reviewed the production a second time when it returned to the Garden Theatre in New York City in April 1903 after a national tour that included several weeks of performances in Boston. Greet continued to revive the production throughout his career. The 1902–3 production seems to have been done with little or no scenery, but a 1913 revival at the Children's Theatre in New York used a lavishly decorated unit set,[15] evidence that Greet's approach to scenery was driven by commercial expediency.

Even though reviewers consistently comment on the success of the simple staging, which obviously derives from Poel's ideas regarding Elizabethan production, none at the time made any connection between *Everyman* and the staging of Shakespeare's plays. The minimalist staging was seen as a medieval feature of the performance.

Greet, who had been touring with outdoor productions of Shakespeare in England during the summer months for almost twenty years, now found himself in America in May at the end of his *Everyman* tour; so he did what was natural for him. With actors from the *Everyman* company he commenced a brief alfresco tour of *As You Like It* and *Comedy of Errors* at a number of eastern universities including Columbia,[16] Princeton,[17] and Harvard. Among the members of the faculty committee that arranged the Harvard performances was George Pierce Baker.[18]

Greet's alfresco productions were the first tours organized to bring professional actors to college campuses in America. American universities were without drama departments and largely without theatre courses, and very few had access to theatre facilities. By being able to perform outdoors or to adapt to any large hall, the Ben Greet Players made theatre accessible to an entire new segment of the population. Their largely minimalist productions of Shakespeare's plays, staged largely without interruptions and without the textual cuts made to accommodate scenery, introduced a generation of college faculty and students to a method of staging that was much closer to Elizabethan practice than anything they could have seen elsewhere in the theatre.

Greet returned to England for the summer of 1903, presumably to oversee the tours of the Ben Greet Players there, and to organize a company for another American tour. In September he and this company were in Berkeley, where he directed Aristophanes' *The Birds* as the inaugural performance of the Hearst Greek Theatre at the University of California. Two days later the company presented *Twelfth Night* in the Greek theatre.

Throughout January of 1904, at Chickering Hall in Boston, Greet presented, in sequence, *Twelfth Night,* in what the program announced was "the Elizabethan manner";[19] a revival of *Everyman*; an amalgam of miracle plays in a medieval setting, billed as *The Star of Bethlehem*; and *The Merchant of Venice*, in a setting based on de Witt's Swan drawing.[20] The company proceeded to the Knickerbocker Theatre in New York, where in February they staged *Twelfth Night* in a setting replicating a portion of the Hall of the Middle Temple in London, where Greet believed that the play had been first presented. Draped doorways up center concealed a small alcove, and a balcony was used for an accompanying organ. The *New York Sunday Telegraph* reviewer noted that Greet had tried and perfected bare staging in open-air productions.[21] In March the company transferred to the Daly Theatre, where they added *As You Like It* to their offerings. The *New York Times* reviewer, presumably John Corbin, wrote that the play had been put on "[w]ith the simple scenic environment which Mr. Greet (and many others) prefer to the pseudo Elizabethan setting of 'Twelfth Night,' which it displaces."[22] These were the first productions in a commercial New York theatre by professional actors in what Greet came to refer to simply as "the Elizabethan manner."[23] Greet's approach for these productions, like Poel's, was not so much to reject scenery as to use the stages on which period plays were first done as settings for proscenium productions.

"Bare staging" is less descriptive of these productions than of three "cheap ticket" performances given on a platform stage for several thousand people a few weeks later at Cooper Union on the New York East Side. Greet was closer to Elizabethan staging conditions when his companies were performing outdoors or in improvised indoor spaces than in Broadway houses. In a *Harper's Weekly* article in 1905, coinciding with Greet's offerings in Mendelssohn Hall, Greet wrote:

> I do not attempt to reproduce the character and dimensions of the Elizabethan Theatre, for our information on the subject is meager and untrustworthy. In fact, I rather desire to avoid the semblance of a Swan Theatre, a Fortune, or a Globe. I would rather imagine the play as being given in one of the college halls, or at Greenwich, Windsor, Whitehall, Hampton Court, or better still, Lincoln's Inn or the Middle Temple. I have purposely designed my stage that I may represent the plays without the distractions of a sixteenth century playhouse: after all, the play is the thing and not the surroundings.[24]

The *New York Times* reviewer compared Greet's Mendelssohn Hall production of *Macbeth* with a Robert Mantell Broadway production running at the same time that used "heavy and picturesque scenic equipment" and armies of supernumeraries. The reviewer noted that Greet's audience, unlike Mantell's, heard the poet's lines read much as they were written "and they were apparently well satisfied."[25]

The "Elizabethan" productions of both Poel and Greet had always been resisted by a contingent contending that such minimalist staging had only antiquarian interest and that modern audiences expected all of the technical trappings of the modern theatre. Lew Sparks Akin, in his 1974 doctoral study of Greet's American tours, maintained that after an unsuccessful 1907 engagement at the Garden Theatre in New York, trying to do simplified staging of Shakespeare, Greet's interest in Elizabethan staging waned.[26] Greet continued to use the phrase "in the Elizabethan manner" to justify low-budget indoor and outdoor touring productions, but he fell back on pictorial scenic conventions whenever he could in order to appeal to an audience for whom the novelty of Elizabethan staging had quickly passed. A *New York Dramatic Mirror* reviewer in 1908 favorably contrasts the "natural style" of Greet's alfresco productions with the less desirable "Elizabethan manner."[27]

After his 1902–3 tour under Charles Frohman, Greet could not obtain bookings with Frohman,[28] so he initiated the concert booking system, then used for the first time in the United States according to Kenneth McGowan in *Footlights across America*.[29] In this system the company is contracted for a flat fee by a local sponsor, who may then charge whatever admission price seems appropriate. This arrangement, still used today to finance concert series, made it fairly easy for colleges or private clubs to book Greet's company.

The company recruited in England in 1904 featured Constance Crawley, who replaced Edith Wynne Matthison as Everyman and in principal women's parts. Her understudy, who increasingly assumed her roles, was Sybil Thorndike, who toured with Greet for three seasons. She later became one of the most prominent of twentieth-century British actresses and Dame Sybil. Her letters written home during this tour were incorporated into her biography written by her brother, Russell, later a member of the company himself. This material gives us the most complete account available for a Greet tour, which this year began on Long Island and then proceeded westward, making stops at Pittsfield, Massachusetts; Rochester and Syracuse, New York; and Chicago before striking out for the University of California, where they staged *Hamlet* in the Hearst Theatre. They then toured the West Coast, going as far north as Vancouver. After Christmas they returned eastward, making

stops for one-night stands in Nevada, Utah, Colorado, Kansas, and Illinois, all indoors but still without scenery. They reopened their outdoor
season in the spring with *The Tempest* at Magill University in Montreal.
In the latter part of June and early July they were at the University of
Cincinnati with a repertory of six Shakespearean plays, ending the tour
with several engagements on the East Coast.[30]

Greet varied the tour somewhat, going, for example, into the Southeast in 1905, but the basic pattern was repeated for the twelve seasons
that he toured the States. He tended to return to localities year after
year, certainly an indication of his popularity. The University of California even offered him a professorship in 1905.[31] A program for Greet's
production of *The Tempest* at Princeton in 1907 gave a "partial list" of
engagements during the company's first five seasons in America: five
private clubs and twenty-four colleges, including the Universities of
Tennessee and Virginia and the University of the South.[32]

Greet's success spurred imitators, most immediately and most successfully Charles Coburn, whose open-air Shakespeare company began
in 1904 with four engagements. At first he concentrated on clubs, perhaps in deference to Greet's head start on a college circuit, but in 1909
Coburn added Percy MacKaye's dramatization of *The Canterbury Tales*
to the company's largely Shakespearean repertory and began to seek
college billings, playing in winter months "with paraphernalia and lighting effects and arranged for presentation in college auditoriums and
halls."[33] By 1914, the year that Greet returned to England, Coburn's
letterhead provides a cumulative list of engagements that includes 92
colleges, and by 1917 that number had increased to 124.[34] In 1916 Coburn had a successful run of a revival of *The Yellow Jacket*, by George C.
Hazelton and Berimo, and thereafter devoted his tours almost exclusively to this play.

Before the First World War half a dozen other outdoor troupes performed classical works with minimalist staging for college audiences,
including a company in 1910 headed by Constance Crawley, who had
been with Greet in 1904,[35] and another organized around P. J. Kelly,
who performed with the Greet Players in 1909.[36] Frank McEntee, who
had been a member of Greet's early American companies and later with
Charles Coburn, started his own outdoor company when Greet left
America in 1914.[37] Another actor, Frank Lee Short, began a company
in 1912 that performed outdoors for several years but not doing Shakespeare. Short had studied with Franklin Sargent at the Empire Dramatic
School and had been in the 1895 production of *Epicoene* at Harvard. In
January of 1903, at Mrs. Osborn's Playhouse in New York City, he had
tried his own production of *Romeo and Juliet* in a reconstructed Swan

theatre with an onstage audience in Elizabethan costumes and placards to indicate changes in locale. The *New York Times* reviewer speculated that the concept might have worked better for a play where the modern audience is not "accustomed by long experience to gorgeous scenery."[38] Short later became the drama coach of the Yale Dramatic Association, where he did outdoor productions of *The Merry Wives of Windsor* in 1909 and *The Taming of the Shrew* in 1910.[39]

Greet returned to America for tours in 1929 and 1930 that included colleges, but he made no attempt to perform outdoors. He seems, however, to have used a setting made of no more than gray curtains. Greet's biographer, Winifred Isaac, transcribes an entry from the diary kept of the 1929–30 tour by Stanford Holme, a member of the company, who complained about a performance in Morgantown, West Virginia: "a perfect horror of a stage with no front curtain—simply a billiards table with curtains at the back and audience *all round* and up to within an inch of the stage—no proper lighting either."[40] Clearly, Greet had not communicated the spirit of the Elizabethan stage to Holme.

In 1911 Greet wrote an article for the *World's Work*, arguing for an American Shakespeare Memorial Theatre accompanied by an acting school. Even though he refers to an earlier letter written to the *Times* (London) calling for "a reproduction of the Globe Theatre in London," he makes no such suggestion for his proposed American theatre.[41] For Greet the revival of Elizabethan staging had been but a passing phase in his lifelong effort to find a popular audience for the presentation of Shakespeare's plays in the manner that he had the resources to stage. Nonetheless, audiences and reviewers continued to associate Greet with what had come to be recognized as "the Elizabethan Revival." A columnist in the *New York Dramatic Mirror* gleefully relates an overheard conversation in which a child recognizes Greet as "Mr. No Scenery."[42]

Greet's assessment of popular taste was correct. In America, as in London, scenic Shakespeare won the day, and productions of Richard Sothern and Julia Marlowe in the early decades of the century continued the elaborate Victorian staging traditions of Richard Mansfield and Robert Mantell. Commercial theatre in the twentieth century had trouble with more than Elizabethan staging of Shakespeare; it had trouble with any staging of Shakespeare. Thus the number of commercial productions of Shakespeare's plays steadily diminished. A counterpoint to this decline was the rise of college productions and the eventual development of Shakespearean festival theatres, most associated with academic institutions.

Poel, Baker, and Greet each had more than an idea; each acted on the vision that he had of Shakespeare's theatre and demonstrated its feasibility and the lost theatrical values thus recovered. None had the power, however, to redirect the tastes of the popular commercial theatre. All gravitated toward an audience that was more "academic" than "commercial," and Greet, particularly, found ways to reach this new audience in large numbers. Some of the first theatrical experiences of the emerging academic theatre were the alfresco or minimalist productions of Shakespeare presented "in the Elizabethan manner" by Greet or his many imitators.[43] Greet may not have so much led the way as followed the scent, but he found an American audience for the Elizabethan Revival.

Notes

1. Esther Dunn, *Shakespeare in America* (New York: Macmillan, 1939), 305.

2. Arthur J. Harris, "William Poel's Elizabethan Stage: The First Experiment," *Theatre Notebook* 17 (1963): 111–14.

3. Reprinted in C. E. Montague, *Dramatic Values* (London: Methuen, 1911), 244.

4. See Richard Foulkes, *Performing Shakespeare in the Age of Empire* (Cambridge, UK: Cambridge University Press, 2002).

5. Wisner Payne Kinne, *George Pierce Baker and the American Theatre* (Cambridge, MA: Harvard University Press, 1954), 58–59.

6. Kinne identifies the source of this production as the American Academy of Dramatic Art (59), but a *New York Times* article identified the performance as having been by the students of the Empire Dramatic School. See "'Twelfth Night' Given without Scenery at the Empire Theatre," *New York Times*, Feb. 21, 1903, 8.

7. Kinne, *George Pierce Baker*, 59.

8. Baker, in *The Development of Shakespeare as a Dramatist* (New York: Macmillan, 1907), cites (n. 99) Cecil Brodmeir, *Die Shakespeare-Bühne nach den alten Bühnenanweisungen.*

9. Cary Mazer, *Shakespeare Refashioned: Elizabethan Plays on Edwardian Stages* (Ann Arbor: University of Michigan Press, 1981), 71.

10. Lew Sparks Akin, "Ben Greet and His Theatre Companies in America: 1902–1932" (PhD diss., University of Georgia, 1974), 29, argues that these productions used "simplified staging," but this appears more a matter of economy than philosophy on Greet's part.

11. Winifred F. E. C. Isaac, *Ben Greet and the Old Vic* (London: Greenbank Press, ca. 1964), 56.

12. Robert Speaight, *William Poel and the Elizabethan Revival* (Cambridge, MA: Harvard University Press, 1954), 104.

13. Speaight mistakenly labels photographs of this production as 1901 (see facing p. 225), but the 1901 productions were presented outside.

14. Speaight, *William Poel*, 162.

15. Isaac, *Ben Greet*, 82.

16. *New York Dramatic Mirror*, May 23, 1903, 3.

17. Program from the Princeton Theatre Collection.

18. Isaac, *Ben Greet*, 86–89.

19. Reprinted in Isaac, *Ben Greet*, 109.

20. *New York Dramatic Mirror*, Feb. 6, 1904, 14.

21. *New York Sunday Telegraph*, Feb. 28, 1904, "Ben Greet" clipping file, Theatre Collection of the New York Public Library, Lincoln Center.

22. *New York Times*, March 15, 1904, 9.

23. Frank Lee Short's production of *Romeo and Juliet* in October 1902 on a reconstructed Swan stage at Mrs. Osborne's Playhouse (see below) may better deserve this distinction. Even though the production was widely reviewed and panned by the New York press, the four-hundred-seat theatre, formerly the Berkeley Lyceum, may not qualify as a Broadway theatre.

24. Ben Greet, *Harper's Weekly*, Nov. 4, 1905, 1604.

25. *New York Times*, Nov. 14, 1905, 9.

26. Akin, "Ben Greet," 131–32.

27. *New York Dramatic Mirror*, June 20, 1908, 9.

28. Milicent Evison, quoted in Isaac, *Ben Greet*, 115.

29. Kenneth McGowan, *Footlights across America* (New York: Harcourt, Brace, 1929), 73.

30. Russell Thorndike, *Sybil Thorndike* (London: Thornton Butterworth, 1929).

31. *New York Times*, Apr. 12, 1905.

32. Princeton Theatre Collection. Several locations mentioned by Thorndike are omitted from this list.

33. L. M. Goodstadt, Coburn's manager, to colleges [1909], Charles Coburn Papers, University of Georgia Library.

34. Charles Coburn Papers.

35. *New York Dramatic Mirror*, Aug. 6, 1910.

36. *New York Dramatic Mirror*, June 10, 1914.

37. Isaac, *Ben Greet*, 102.

38. *New York Times*, "Shakespeare in the Ark," Jan. 28, 1903, 9.

39. Programs in Yale Theatre Collection.

40. Isaac, *Ben Greet*, 195.

41. Reprinted in Isaac, *Ben Greet*, 119–25.

42. *New York Dramatic Mirror*, Apr. 26, 1911, 4.

43. See Richard H. Palmer, "The Professional Actor's Early Search for a College Audience: Sir Philip Ben Greet and Charles Coburn," *Educational Theatre Journal* 21, no. 1 (Mar. 1969): 51–59.

The Spaces between Now and Then

Historiography of the Body and Stage-Centered Studies of Combat on the Shakespearean Stage

Aaron Anderson

THE FIELD OF theatre history has recently moved away from wholesale reliance on text-based research to include what have become known as stage-centered or performance-based methodologies. Recreations of historical theatre spaces such as the "rebuilt" Globe in London or the "reproduced" Blackfriars Playhouse in Staunton, Virginia, are part of this trend. Among the more obvious benefits that such spaces hold for theatre historians is the ability to "embody" theories of past staging practices: to experiment with and to experience some of the problems and possibilities faced by actors now long since gone, to metaphorically walk in the footsteps of the past. In this sense replicated stage spaces may become methodological tools used to reconstruct bits of the past itself. Yet there is a strange juxtaposition of diachronic and synchronic models of history that often goes unnoticed in such stage-centered investigations, a juxtaposition caused by the fundamental yet often unstated differences in the two trusts of stage-centered historical research: on the one hand, reconstructed architecture can replicate the three dimensions of space (height, depth, and width) from a particular point in time, but, on the other hand, the bodies used to replicate movement within that space carry many cultural inscriptions beyond that singular historical moment.

Although few will deny that walking in the footsteps of the past is not the same thing as walking with the feet of the past, only a handful of researchers have fully acknowledged the methodological consequences of this distinction. This lack of concern is largely due to the fact that, at first glance, the body itself seems wholly biological (or *natu-*

ral as the term is often used), and therefore modern bodies seem largely the same as past bodies. Yet, in fact, all bodies—whether onstage or not—are shaped, conditioned, and responsive to more than just biology. Every movement of the body is informed and habituated by cultural forces as well. This means that countless cultural inscriptions influence the movement patterns of modern reconstructions in very fundamental— yet often unstated—ways. In other words, even though they move through replicated spaces, modern bodies used to recreate past movements do not actually replicate the movement patterns of any singular point in time but are rather linked to many moments and many spaces. In fact, any description of the body must include many more elements than simply the dimensions of space and time. Even a static body reflects nuances of gender, race, nationality, age, and sexuality (to name but a few defining characteristics); whereas a moving body multiplies the complexity of any useful description exponentially (including a number of concepts—such as weight, flow, rhythm, cadence, carriage; not to mention inspiration, passion, desire, objective, obstacle, and all the other elements of modern acting often taken for granted as entirely biological or "natural"—that many movement scholars consider fundamental). However, these cultural distinctions are not always readily apparent, and the biology of the body is too often used as the entire description. This can, unfortunately, lead to generalized—and thus dehistoricizing—assumptions about the ways in which modern bodies can inform us about the past. As a way of demonstrating some of the dangers that generalized assumptions about the body have for stage-centered investigations, I will first describe a few of the assumptions that have already been made about replications of historical combat on modern stages and then outline a number of points that I believe must be addressed in order to develop a more useful historiography of movement.

Of Swords and Stages: Reading the Moving Body

The theatre research topic most concerned with recreating movement on replicated stages or with replicated props involves questions of how the fights in Shakespeare's plays were originally staged. Yet, ironically, few researchers in this area have acknowledged any methodological complexity in their topic. This is especially problematic because the difficulty of reconstructing past movement is only made even more complex when the movement in question is defined by only two words from any one of a number of plays: "they fight." Because of the obvious ambiguity of these stage directions, scholars trying to recreate the movement they describe have often looked to a variety of other evidence sources. They have looked, for example, at much longer and more detailed stage directions such as, "In scuffling they change Rapiers,"[1] or to other clues in the text such as Benvolio's description:

> Of [*Tybalt*] deaf to peace, but that he Tilts
> With Piercing steel at bold *Mercutio's* breast,
> Who, all as hot, turns deadly point to point,
> And, with [Martial] scorn, with one hands [beats]
> Cold death aside, and with the other sends
> It back to Tybalt, whose dexterity
> Retorts it . . .[2]

In order to move beyond the limitations of the play texts, scholars also looked to period English-language fencing manuals or to descriptions of contemporaneous gladiatorial fencing exhibitions;[3] and as stage-centered studies of Shakespearean performance gained acceptance within the academies, a number of scholars have also used their own practical stage experience as evidence to support theories of historical movement.

Use of this last type of movement evidence is what performance scholar Joseph Roach describes as "[juxtaposing] living memory as restored behavior against a historical archive of scripted records" and what dance scholar Susan Foster describes as "writing" the "historian's . . . body" into the text.[4] In line with the general trend toward stage-centered studies of history, both Roach and Foster see such linking "between past and present bodies" as methodological movement in the right direction.[5] Yet Roach and Foster are also two of the few scholars who have wrestled with the methodological consequences of this approach. Thus Roach focuses the bulk of his own investigation on questions of memory and forgetting within a longer historical and material continuum, and Foster argues at length that any juxtaposition of present and past bodies must "take shape from the formal constraints imposed by the discipline of history," including "interpretation of their role in the cultural production of meaning."[6] Unfortunately, the authors of the three most recent books on the history of combat on the Shakespearean stage—Craig Turner and Tony Soper, Charles Edelman, and Joseph Martinez—do not take such pains.[7] Instead, these authors simply juxtapose present movement practices with imagined "bodies" from the past, without taking into account the complex methodological implications such practice carries with it.

Turner and Soper, Edelman, and Martinez all describe similar research goals—analysis of historical staging conditions and culture in order to influence modern staging practice—and the methods of historical analysis in their works likewise also include elements of present performance to inform readings of the past. Of the three, Edelman is the clearest on this point: "In the absence of other textual or historical evidence . . . I will occasionally look to the modern theatre, and to my own experience, for indications of Elizabethan staging—although some conventions have changed since Shakespeare's day, such as the use of female actors and controlled lighting, the most important theatrical conventions are common to all periods and genres of drama."[8]

Likewise, Turner and Soper occasionally refer to "practical experience on the authors' part," and Martinez uses a mixture of historical analysis and practical experience to construct modern choreography.[9] Juxtaposing the bodies of modern practitioners with historical textural evidence in this manner does allow these and other authors to investigate questions beyond the purview of written evidence alone. However, by restricting their samples of movement to two points—a supposed original staging and modern practice—all of these authors essentialize their descriptions of movement even as they attempt to locate this movement within a specific historical context.

"Shakespearean Performance," although often described in universalizing terms, is not, and never was, monolithic. The analysis of movement in Turner and Soper's, Edelman's, and Martinez's works focuses primarily on the outdoor, or public, theatre spaces; yet we know that Shakespeare's plays were written for and performed in a variety of other spaces as well, including the indoor (second) Blackfriars Playhouse, the Inns of Court, and unknown numbers of university and tavern halls.[10] Complicating this further is the fact that modern editions of the plays are themselves often the compilations of modern editors and, as such, may reflect the influence of the long history of editing practice and canonization. This ongoing "historical inscription" is true of the performance texts as well.[11] A vast amount of recent scholarship demonstrates that present productions of Shakespeare's plays derive as much from the long history of performance tradition—and the changes therein—as from any supposed "original" staging. Rather, modern Shakespearean practice derives from a long history of passions, acting points, proscenium stages, neo-Elizabethanism, actor-management, the rise of modern directors, and the history of Shakespearean criticism itself—to name but a few of the influences. Each of these, in turn, was often the result of some type of break with the conventions of the immediate past rather than a movement backward toward an "original" past. The result of this long historical inscription is that universalizing generalizations about performance history—such as Edelman's contention that the most important theatrical conventions are common to all periods and genres—are more likely to obscure relevant facts than illuminate specific staging practices.

Understanding the implications of ongoing processes of historical inscription is especially important when considering present movement practice as a window into the movement practices of the past; for if a historian's body is understood to incorporate "predilections" of bodies from the past—traces of history inscribed in the fabric of present movement—then this inscription must also be understood as carrying traces not only from a single given historical moment but also as carrying traces from the longer history of the movement form itself.[12] Failure to recognize this is related to what dance scholar Andrée Grau has called "myths of origins" and the "universalist fallacy," which are, in dance theories, essentializing notions that dance in all its myriad cultural forms developed in some monolithic, prehistorical ur-culture in order to express the universal biological needs of our essential selves.[13] Although Grau's criticism is directed at universalizing theories of the "origins" of dance, something of these same essentializing myths informs modern theories of the combat on Shakespeare's "original" stages.

Let me illustrate this with a few examples. There was a time in England when displays of sport and theatrical productions were performed on the same stages. In particular, the remnants of a fencing monopoly known as the "Masters of Defense" made their prizefights public for increased publicity and revenue by holding their bouts in public spaces, including the then-new outdoor public playhouses. Scholars researching the history of combat on the stage have seized on this sharing of venues as evidence that the sword fighting in Elizabethan and Jacobean plays—especially Shakespeare's—and the sports combat of the Masters' prizefights must have shared a common performance aesthetic.[14] The basic premise of this argument is that the audiences for both types of performance—sports and theatre—and their expectations regarding the performance of sword fights must have been at least partially the same because of the sharing of venues and the use of similar weapons. Yet this argument is difficult to sustain. For instance, a contemporary analogous argument might be to say that since the hand-to-hand combat in both Disney's *Beauty and the Beast on Ice* and the no-holds-barred *Ultimate Fighting Championships* is often performed in the same coliseum spaces, the audiences must overlap to some extent and will necessarily hold the combat in *Beauty and the Beast* to the same aesthetics as that found in the "ultimate fighting."

Other scholars have pointed to the fact that Richard Tarleton, the great comic actor of the Queen's Men, was himself a Master of Defense.[15] As Arthur Wise writes in *Weapons in the Theatre*: "it seems likely that the spectators at his Masters prize . . . would also be part of the audience for his play performance. . . . Such audiences would make the highest demands regarding the execution of theatrical fights since they would have specialist experience of combat between the most skilled exponents in the country.[16]

However, this also inadvertently points out the fact that none of the leading tragedians of the day appear to have held this same status within the fencing fraternity (or at least there is no evidence to support that they did). If the aesthetics of combat for both the Masters' prizes and the sword fighting in the plays was indeed the same, then it would make much more sense for a man such as Richard Burbage—who performed in most of Shakespeare's history and tragedy combat scenes—rather than Tarleton, a comic, to be able to perform fights with "[spectacular]" realism.[17] Indeed, given the prevalence of combat in many tragedies and histories, and the lack of such combat in most comedies, the Master status of Tarleton is more likely to be coincidence than planned aesthetic. That is, the fact that a leading comedian was an expert fencer probably says more about the general culture of the times than it does about the specific performance aesthetic of combat on the stage.

The idea of shared venues as evidence of shared aesthetics also supposes a basically homogeneous audience, yet almost everything that we presently know about Elizabethan audiences suggests that they were probably "much more evidently heterogeneous in demeanor, dress, behavior, and social privilege than audiences today."[18] Performance in the same space, in the same city, even if held on consecutive nights, does not necessarily equate to overlap in audience; and, even if we do assume some degree of audience overlap between sporting exhibitions and theatrical performances, there is still no compulsory basis to assume that the aesthetics of audience reception must necessarily be the same for both events. Yet this argument is echoed in some way by nearly every researcher writing in the field of the history of combat on Shakespearean stages, including Turner and Soper, Edelman, Martinez, and many others.[19]

This impulse to universalize audience response is directly at odds with the insistence on contextual particularity that governs most current approaches to performance history. Yet I believe that these historiographical inconsistencies are not motivated by lapses in logic but, rather, by failure to take into account the fact that movement forms are themselves nonmonolithic constructs and are subject to the same processes of historical inscription and contextual particularity as both written and performance texts. Looking at samples of movement in addition to a supposed "original" Shakespearean moment and present practice may serve as a strategy to offset this "universalist fallacy" of movement forms.

Consider, for example, the Restoration stage: a period when "Shakespearean performance" broke with the conventions of its immediate—or at least pre–civil war—past, a period when Shakespeare was deliberately "[reformed]" and made to "[fit]" the new aesthetics of the times.[20] As a result of this reform many scenes of combat were conducted offstage or done away with altogether. For instance, and in direct contrast to Arthur Wise's observation that *Romeo and Juliet* "contains some of the most spectacular fighting scenes of any Elizabethan play," the Restoration adaptation of this play by Thomas Otway, *Caius Marius*, contains hardly any fighting spectacle at all.[21] Although the sword fights in Shakespeare's "original" *Romeo and Juliet* probably added to the visual spectacle, in *Caius Marius* either there was a lesser desire for such spectacle or something else—such as the (then) new scene houses and movable scenery—had taken its place in performance.

Possibly as a result of the intricacies of this movable scenery, Restoration theatres do not seem to have served the same dual purpose as venues for both theatrical plays and gladiatorial combats as did their outdoor predecessors; and in the journals of Samuel Pepys we have evidence of a person who did, in fact, attend both the gladiatorial exhibitions and theatrical plays of his day. Yet contrary to a theory of shared aesthetics, Pepys's journals indicate that he judged each type of performance by very different standards. His descriptions of the content of plays include a wide variety of visual and presentational aesthetics unrelated to the performance of combat. He writes:

> *December 28, 1666:* . . . saw *Henry the Fifth* well done by the Duke's people, and in most excellent habits, all new vests, being put on but this night. . . .
>
> *January 7, 1667:* To the Duke's house, and saw *Macbeth*, which though I saw it lately, yet appears a most excellent play in all respects, but especially in divertisment, though it be a deep tragedy; which is a strange perfection in tragedy, it being most proper here, and suitable.
>
> *April 19, 1667:* To the play-house, where we saw *Macbeth*, which, though I have seen it often, yet it is one of the best plays for a stage, and variety of dancing and music, that ever I saw.
>
> *January 3, 1668:* . . . to the play *The Tempest*, which we have often seen, but yet I was pleased again. . . . [I]t is so full of variety, and particularly this day I took pleasure to learn the tune of the seaman's dance.[22]

The aesthetic concern in these entries revolves around almost neoclassic, "sophisticated" visual and aural pleasures such as "new vests," "divertisment," the "proper and suitable" form of tragedy, and the "tune of the dance."

These theatrical concerns contrast directly with Pepys's vivid accounts of the gladiatorial combats he witnessed. He writes:

> We went to see such a combat, which was performed on a stage in the middle of an amphitheater, when, on the flourish of trumpets and the beat of drums, the combatants entered, stripped to their shirts. On a signal from the drum, they drew their swords and immediately began to fight, skirmishing a long time without wounds. They were both very skillful and courageous. The tallest had the advantage over the smallest, for, according to the English fashion of fencing, they endeavored rather to cut than to thrust in the French manner, so that by his height he had the advantage of being able to strike his antagonist on the head, against which the little one was on his guard. He had in his turn one advantage over the tall man in being able to give him the Jarnac stroke, by cutting him on the right ham, which he left in a manner quite unguarded. So that, all things considered, they were equally matched. Nevertheless, the tall one struck the little one on the wrist, which he almost cut off, but this did not prevent him from continuing the fight, after he had been dressed, and taken a glass or two of wine to give him courage, when he took ample vengeance for his wound; for a little afterwards, making a feint at the ham, the tall man stooping in order to parry it, laid his whole head open, when the little man gave him a stroke which took off a slice of his head and almost all his ear. For my part, I think there is a barbarity and inhumanity in permitting men to kill each other for diversion. The surgeons immediately dressed them and bound up their wounds; which being done, they renewed the combat, and both being sensible of their respective disadvantages, they therefore went a long time without receiving or giving a wound, which was the cause that the little one, failing to parry so exactly, being tired with his long battle, received another stroke on his wounded wrist, which, dividing the sinews, he remained vanquished.[23]

The contrast between the descriptions of both types of performance is significant: the combat in the plays goes unmentioned, whereas that in the gladiatorial bouts is described in great detail. The "proper" performance of tragedy in Pepys's description is clearly removed from the "barbarity and inhumanity" of the prizefights. And, likewise, what attracted the crowds to the "diversion" of sports combat seems to have had little to do with the appeal of the sophisticated, "proper divertisment" of the stage plays. In essence, what we find by looking beyond a supposed "original" moment is that the two types of performances—stage plays and gladiatorial combats—may not have been judged by the same aesthetic standards in "all periods and genres" as Edelman's contention seems to imply.

This division of aesthetics does not, of course, necessarily tell us anything about the Elizabethan and Jacobean periods, but it might allow us to revisit the theory of earlier shared aesthetics with the idea that all sword fighting—even within the same historical period, or performed with similar weapons, or on similar stages—is not necessarily the same movement form. We might then begin to ask more informed questions about the significance of shared venues in relation to perceptions of movement. As a number of dance scholars have pointed out, understanding how to "read . . . movement" ironically often involves paying attention to issues of "textuality."[24] Thus, movement "texts," just as other texts, may be thought of as existing in discourse, so a movement text such as a "prizefight" may have something to say to and about other movement texts such as a "stage fight," but this discourse, this similarity, does not make these texts the same. Yet most of the descriptions of combat on Elizabethan and Jacobean stages analytically conflate these two forms. This is problematic since conflating similarity with sameness may erase potentially useful distinctions between the two forms.

Of all the scholars writing on this subject only Alan Dessen takes into consideration the possibility of differing aesthetics for stage as opposed to sports exhibitions, and he has suggested that the player's stage fights may have been conducted through a shared vocabulary of theatrical conventions—what he calls "the logic of stage violence"—rather than through anything corresponding directly to the movement of the Masters' prizefights.[25] However—and in keeping with necessary skepticism of scholarly debate—Cary Mazer, in turn, has argued that Dessen's own interpretation owes much to the particular historical moment of the 1970s and the rise of the modern director's theatre.[26] Such criticism does not invalidate Dessen's theory; however, arguments such as Mazer's do convincingly point out that many current theories of past performance practice necessarily include traces of the present. This, in turn, raises valid concerns about methods of historiography and the need to historicize modern theories of the past. In a similar vein I suggest this same scrutiny has yet to be applied to modern theories of combat on Shakespearean stages.

In other words, the theories put forward in the 1990s by Turner and Soper, Edelman, and Martinez that link the aesthetics of Masters' prizefights with those of theatrical stage fights may reflect as much, if not more, about the present moment as they do about the actual practices of the past. For, if history or "remembering" is, as Homi Bhabha writes, "a putting together of the dismembered past,"[27] then we should never lose sight of the fact that the original or authentic in this past may be in some ways forever lost to us through this very dismemberment and that the act of choosing which elements to "re-member," or reconstruct, in our historical narratives may often—if not fundamentally—also include political acts masquerading within our epistemological questions. In this light present searches for historical connections between fencers and players might also involve a modern desire for legitimization within the field of stage-combat research—as Edelman, Martinez, Turner, and Soper all also work as professional fight directors—or it may simply be an aspect of the sheer weight of research tradition linking these two forms. In any event the use of present movement as a method of reconstructing the past necessarily implicates the historicized particularity—the "bodies" if you will—of historians such as Turner and Soper, Edelman, and Martinez within the very movement they seek to reconstruct. Yet none of these authors attend to this implication of the methodology.

Toward a Historiography of Movement Forms

Until now I have avoided as much as possible using the phrase "the body" as a way to describe methods of movement analysis for fear that the phrase itself may veil aspects of what I am trying to describe.[28] By invoking it now, I am trying to draw attention to three interrelated points about the use of present bodies and their movements as methodological tools used to reconstruct past bodies and movements. First, movement texts—even if performed on the same stages, or with similar props (such as weapons), or for the same audiences, or, for that matter, with the same bodies—may not necessarily be the same text, and the only way to even consider this possibility is to avoid descriptions of movement forms as "essentially" the same. Second, the inclusion of modern bodies within any historical analysis necessitates first and foremost paying attention to the historical particularity of the present moment. This has an added benefit of possibly lessening universalist tendencies implicit in theories of "the body" by historicizing the discourse and locating it within a particular, contextualized "body." In this way we might also then be able to approach the usually unasked questions of why a particular narrative of history is emphasized in the first place, who is writing the narratives, and what other possible acts may lurk within the questions. And finally, thinking of present movement forms as carrying traces of the past requires that we also conceive of these traces as having been continually inscribed throughout the longer history of the movement form. This means that the samples of movement—the bodies—that we choose to analyze should include examples from the history of the movement in addition to the particular moment we wish to consider. This need not imply that any present movement represents an unbroken line of transmission from the past or that movement forms are not themselves broken and disjointed texts. It simply implies that if present movement practices are theorized as carrying historical inscriptions, then these inscriptions necessarily include moments beyond any—possibly mythic—original, and realizing this may be one way to lessen universalist fallacies. In other words, each of these points requires the additional admission that any investigation into the past must be conducted using the tools, biases, and bodies of the present and that this present may include traces of the past beyond the limitations of the two moments—then and now—under consideration.

By noting all of this, I do not mean to suggest that modern stage-centered studies of movement in recreated spaces have nothing to tell us about the past or that recreations of historical performances on modern stages are merely reflections of current desires. What I am suggesting, rather, is simply that modern recreations of past movement practices are always and necessarily products of more than one point in time. Thus any modern body attempting to recreate movement from the past necessarily engages in the creation of a new entity: a unique movement that is representative of neither merely the present nor merely the past but is rather a complex hybrid composed of many times and many "bodies." The methodological danger is simply that this is not always self-evident, for—as dance scholars have noted for years—the complexity of the body is often veiled by its supposed naturalness. The best way to see behind this veil then is, first, to recognize that it is there. Only once we recognize this can we begin to come to terms with the juxtapositions inherent in stage-centered research practices by treating any "recreated" movement with the same skepticism that underlies all other historiographical investigations. For it is only in this skepticism that we may find the rigorous methodologies necessary to truly advance our understanding.

Notes

1. William Shakespeare, *Mr. William Shakespeares Comedies, Histories, & Tragedies. Published According to the True Original Copies* (1623; reprinted in

facsimile edition as *The First Folio of Shakespeare 1623* [New York: Applause Books, 1995], 771).

2. Shakespeare, *First Folio*, 663.

3. Although this area of scholarship is well established, the methodology of using martial evidence to support theories of stage movement has rarely been examined.

4. Joseph Roach, *Cities of the Dead: Circum-Atlantic Performance* (New York: Columbia University Press, 1996), 11; Susan Leigh Foster, introduction to *Choreographing History*, ed. Susan Leigh Foster (Bloomington: Indiana University Press, 1995), 7.

5. Foster, *Choreographing History*, 7–8.

6. Ibid.

7. See Craig Turner and Tony Soper, *Methods and Practice of Elizabethan Swordplay* (Carbondale: Southern Illinois University Press, 1990); Charles Edelman, *Brawl Ridiculous: Swordfighting in Shakespeare's Plays* (New York: Manchester University Press, 1992); J. D. Martinez, *The Swords of Shakespeare: An Illustrated Guide to Stage Combat Choreography in the Plays of Shakespeare* (Jefferson, NC: McFarland, 1996). Although Turner and Soper's *Methods* is outwardly concerned more with the recreation of sword play itself (as opposed to strictly Shakespearean sword play), the book makes numerous references to Shakespearean performance, performers, and spaces, and the biographies of both men list only their theatrical—not fencing—credentials.

8. Edelman, *Brawl Ridiculous*, 10.

9. Turner and Soper, *Methods*, 71.

10. Turner and Soper do draw attention to an indoor space that later became the second Blackfriars Playhouse in order to highlight connections between this space, fencers, and stage players; yet in doing so they often overstate the point by closely juxtaposing examples of sword play that are otherwise unrelated; for instance, in a paragraph otherwise concerned only with the Blackfriars theatre space, they include the description of a duel between John Day and playwright Henry Porter (see ibid., 19).

11. James Bulman, ed., *Shakespeare, Theory, and Performance* (London: Routledge, 1996), 2.

12. Foster, *Choreographing History*, 7.

13. Andrée Grau, "Myths of Origins," in *The Routledge Dance Studies Reader*, ed. Alexandra Carter (London: Routledge, 1998).

14. See also, e.g., James L. Jackson, introduction to *Three Elizabethan Fencing Manuals: Giacomo di Grassi, His True Arte of Defence (1594), Vincent Saviolo, His Practice (1595), George Silver, Paradoxes of Defence (1599) and Bref Instructions upon My Paradoxes of Defence* (New York: Scholars' Facsimiles & Reprints, 1972); Robert E. Morsberger, *Swordplay and the Elizabethan and Jacobean Stage* (Salzburg: Institut für Englische Sprache und Literatur, 1974); Sergio Rossi, "Duelling in the Italian Manner: The Case of *Romeo and Juliet*," in *Shakespeare's Italy: Functions of Italian Locations in Renaissance Drama*, ed. Michele Marrapodi, A. J. Hoenselaars, Marcello Cappuzzo, and Falzon Santucci (Manchester: Manchester University Press, 1993), 112–24; A. Forbes Sieveking,

"Fencing and Duelling," in *Shakespeare's England: An Account of the Life & Manners of His Age,* vol. 2 (Oxford: Clarendon Press, 1916), 389–407; Adolph L. Soens, "Cudgels and Rapiers: The Staging of the Edgar-Oswald Fight in *Lear,*" *Shakespeare Studies* 5 (1969): 149–58; Adolph L. Soens, "Tybalt's Spanish Fencing in *Romeo and Juliet,*" *Shakespeare Quarterly* 20, no. 2 (1969): 121–27; James Taylor, "The Influence of Rapier Fencing on *Hamlet,*" *Forum for Modern Language Studies* 29, no. 3 (1993): 203–15; J. Dover Wilson, introduction to *Paradoxes of Defence,* by George Silver (1599; repr. Oxford: Oxford University Press, 1933); Arthur Wise, *Weapons in the Theatre* (New York: Barnes and Noble, 1968); and Louis B. Wright, "Stage Duelling in the Elizabethan Theatre," *Modern Language Review* 22 (1927): 265–75.

15. See, e.g., Edelman, *Brawl Ridiculous,* 4; Martinez, *Swords,* 1, 21; Morsberger, *Swordplay,* 60; and Turner and Soper, *Methods,* 17.

16. Wise, *Weapons,* 9.

17. Ibid., 8.

18. Bulman, *Shakespeare,* 18.

19. See, e.g., Jackson, *Three Manuals;* Morsberger, *Swordplay;* Rossi, "Duelling"; Sieveking, "Fencing"; Soens, "Cudgels"; Soens, "Tybalt's Spanish Fencing"; Taylor, "Influence"; Wilson, *Paradoxes;* Wise, *Weapons;* and Wright, "Stage Duelling."

20. Sandra Clark, introduction to *Shakespeare Made Fit: Restoration Adaptations of Shakespeare,* ed. Sandra Clark (London: J. M. Dent, 1997), xlii.

21. Wise, *Weapons,* 8.

22. Quoted in Gamini Salgado, *Eyewitnesses of Shakespeare: First Hand Accounts of Performance, 1590–1890* (London: Sussex University Press, 1975), 51–53.

23. Quoted in Arthur Wise, *The Art and History of Personal Combat* (New York: Arma Press, 1971), 126.

24. Heidi Gilpin, "Shaping Critical Spaces: Issues in the Dramaturgy of Movement Performance," in *Dramaturgy in American Theatre: A Source Book,* ed. Susan Jonas, Geoff Proehl, and Michael Lupu (Fort Worth: Harcourt Brace, 1997), 85–86.

25. Alan C. Dessen, *Elizabethan Stage Conventions and Modern Interpreters* (Cambridge, UK: Cambridge University Press, 1984), 105–29.

26. Cary Mazer, "Historicizing Alan Dessen: Scholarship, Stagecraft, and the 'Shakespeare Revolution,'" in Bulman, *Shakespeare,* 149–67.

27. Homi K. Bhabha, *The Location of Culture* (London: Routledge, 1994), 63.

28. The phrase is at once limiting and overdetermined. On the one hand, the "body" suggests merely the biological fact of life without reference to culture; whereas, on the other hand, as the root and location of all need and desire, "the body" as jargon is sometimes overused to the point that all distinctions are dissolved, and the phrase ceases to represent anything at all.

Hannibal Hamlet

Mark Twain, Dan Rice, and *Huckleberry Finn*

David Carlyon

I N *Huckleberry Finn* Mark Twain painted an enduring portrait of old-time Shakespearean performance. As Huck and Jim float their raft down the Mississippi River, they take on two passengers, both charlatans. One has worked scams in mesmerism, phrenology, lecturing, and selling snake oil, whereas the other has swindled as a doctor, fortune teller, and preacher. Joining forces, the rogues decide to fleece the rubes by posing as classical actors, so the first teaches the second his "Hamlet's Soliloquy":

> To be or not to be; that is the bare bodkin
> That makes calamity of so long life;
> For who would fardels bear, till Birnam Wood do come to Dunsinane,
> But that the fear of something after death
> Murders the innocent sleep,
> Great nature's second course,
> And makes us rather sling the arrows of outrageous fortune
> Than fly to others that we know not of.
> . . .
> . . . But soft you, the fair Ophelia:
> Ope not thy ponderous and marble jaws,
> But get thee to a nunnery—go! (Chapter 21)

With this bit of folderol Twain not only sketched two quack performers and a dim-witted audience that would blindly accept such nonsense as the real thing, but he also suggested that this picture is representative of performance before the Civil War. Behind Huck's narration we sense the omniscient writer applying his long experience to satirize the awful performances he had seen as a boy. And the portrait has endured, blending Twain's skill and a sense that we are seeing antebellum life as it was genuinely lived.[1]

Yet what if the picture has been upside down all this time? What if Twain, rather than lampooning bad performers and dull audiences, instead *copied* lampoons he had seen good performers offer alert audiences? That does not diminish his achievement; all writers mold their material, few as well as Twain. But flipping the usual interpretation provides us with a fresh look at the age that nurtured him, at his possible sources, and at his great book.

Twain published *Huckleberry Finn* in 1885 to please his readers in the 1880s. That truism of historiography is obvious yet easy to forget because the image he created of the 1850s is so vivid that it seems to be a historical account. His description of a circus in chapter 22 is often treated that way, as if it were an eyewitness report. Nevertheless, Twain was writing to fit notions he shared with his late-nineteenth-century readers about the pre–Civil War era. In historians' terms his novel is secondary evidence about antebellum events but primary evidence about Gilded Age beliefs. Consider the book's renowned criticism of slavery. That would have been a bold stance as the Civil War began, when most of the country thought abolitionists were dangerous crackpots—and when Twain enlisted in the Confederate Army—but a quarter century after abolition, opposition to slavery was a retrospective comfort for white Americans who saw themselves as progressive. Similarly, with pre–Civil War performance Twain gave his audience the image they desired. He distorted what he had seen for the same reason liars, lovers, and poets distort: to make things appear better. With his depiction of bastardized Shakespeare he manufactured what his creation, Huck, would call a "stretcher" to flatter his readers, abetting them in seeing themselves as more cultured than their predecessors. That aim for status was also true of Twain himself, who struggled to be taken seriously, chafing against the prejudice that his work was trifling because it was comic and written in vernacular. Disparaging the rural past enhanced his stance of sophistication. A professional matter, it was also personal for Twain. As a recent biographer points out, Sam Clemens invented the persona "Mark Twain" to distance himself from the insecurity of his Hannibal past as a "cowed, uncertain, and underdeveloped boy-man."[2]

The presumption of dreadful antebellum performance that Twain helped create continues. Current conventional wisdom holds as articles of faith that old-time performers were mostly bad; that even the best, like Edwin Forrest, were excessive, histrionic, and relied on rant; that the popular genre of melodrama was mediocre and Shakespearean productions shallow; and that audiences were too crude to tell the difference. Despite much fine scholarship on nineteenth-century performance, the traditional notion persists that our ancestors swooned naively for the sappy endings of hackneyed melodrama, when they were not gape-mouthed rubes too ignorant to realize they were watching a play. Their passion for Shakespeare, with enthusiasm and regular attendance greater than our own, has been discounted, twisted to confirm the bias that they were a rowdy rabble only attracted by the crude bits. Even scholars taking fresh looks at our past have difficulty transcending years of acculturation and apologize for Forrest's ranting and shrug at presumably crude audiences. The fundamental historiographic principle, that objects of study should be treated with the same respect we grant ourselves, gets shouldered aside. Sneering or fondly doting, the twenty-first century condescends.[3]

Antebellum performance was more sophisticated than that. It was intelligent, lively, and pertinent to daily lives. Audience involvement was no blundering gaucherie but helped create the performance *and* improve its quality. Bad actors knew they had to improve; good actors knew they could not wallow in indulgence. Our age honors quiet audiences appreciating literary values or political fare but forgets the cost. Now, if an audience does not like a performance, status as sophisticated theatregoers requires silent endurance, on the presumption that theatre professionals stand above their audiences, doling out artistry or political challenge. On the rare occasion that someone does speak up, circular reasoning confirms that *this* audience cannot appreciate the vaunted artistry or is frightened by the supposed challenge. A century and a half ago, however, eager audiences joined in partnership over the footlights to meet, match, and prod quality and challenge.[4]

That especially applied to productions of their favorite playwright, Shakespeare. As Lawrence Levine points out in *Highbrow/Lowbrow*, the idea that Shakespeare is an elite taste requiring special training or at least elevated sensitivity only developed late in the nineteenth century. In the mid-1800s, by contrast, Shakespeare was vastly popular. With no competing pull from television, rock concerts, or team sports, people of all walks of life regularly attended his plays. To assert that an average bootblack or tinker or hod carrier understood Shakespeare better than a professor today may seem patently false, yet historical evidence of regular attendance makes the assertion arguable, especially considering the axiom that Shakespeare's plays are appreciated better in performance than reading. In our own day live experience with the plays is limited, as few see more than a couple of productions annually, and even Shakespeare scholars may attend no more than a dozen a year. Contrast that to the antebellum bootblack who may have seen a dozen productions a *month*, returning to the same plays and actors in a favorite role. Familiarity gave those audiences strong, well-grounded opinions, which they were happy to share aloud in the performance moment.[5]

That performance moment occurred in other sites than we now consider "theatre." Meeting rooms, riverboats (before "showboats"), lecture halls and theatres billed as "lecture rooms," taverns, circuses—any place where a crowd could be gathered played host to full-length plays and shorter scripted pieces. (The term *host* is particularly apt here because our use of *entertainment* evolved in the nineteenth century from innkeepers and tavern keepers "entertaining" their guests. That made it a counterweight to "art," which was simultaneously developing its own specialized connotation, derived from its original meaning of "craft.")[6] Circus sites themselves varied. In the winter, when the weather prevented touring and most circus performers returned to other jobs, all-star shows held forth in theatres in the nation's major cities, including scripted pieces in their offerings. The same theatre in New York or Philadelphia or New Orleans that featured an acting troupe one week might switch to a circus troupe the next. Then in the summer, on tour under canvas tents over sawdust rings, circuses presented more scripted work, including Shakespeare. Later, into and through the Civil War, venues began to specialize, circuses presenting fewer plays and theatres presenting fewer circus acts during plays. Yet until that split became definite, the overlap continued.

Parodies contributed to the lively mix. Discussing the "Hamlet's Soliloquy" in *Huckleberry Finn*, the editors of Twain's collected works, Walter Blair and Victor Fischer, point out that Shakespeare parodies were a staple of nineteenth-century theatre. Parodies regularly popped up in circuses, particularly in their Shakespearean clowns. The British circus historian George Speaight estimates that the vogue for this variation on the talking clown lasted from the mid-1830s to the mid-1860s. Evidence of what Shakespearean clowns actually said and did is difficult to find because most of it was performed on the fly in an oral age. Clowns varied their basic routines based on what an individual audience did, and that creative interaction of variation and contribution is inevitably lost to history. Speaight made a study of the foremost English example, William F. Wallett, and could only deduce that this self-styled Queen's jester employed "authentic Shakespearean humor." Advertisements and newspaper notices in America rarely provide details but suggest that clown use fluctuated from brief quotations to full-blown parodies. The circus was a horse-based amusement, so the line from *Richard III*, "My horse, my horse, my kingdom for a horse," was perfect

Dan Rice in 1849. Daguerreotype, Thomas M. Easterly, Missouri Historical Society, St. Louis.

for introducing a riding act. Act 5 of that play was itself presented in the ring.[7]

In the United States the foremost Shakespearean clown, Dan Rice, was also the greatest clown of his day—and perhaps the greatest American clown ever. He began as a solo act around 1840, venturing to the Mississippi valley to try his hand, like Twain's charlatans, at mesmerism, lecturing, preaching, and acting—anything to get on in the world but avoid humdrum daily life. Starting in the circus in 1843, Rice appeared as a comic singer; as a knockabout clown; in costume as an actor in scenes; in blackface at a time when circuses regularly sported whiteface and blackface clowns, before minstrelsy migrated from the circus into its own form; and ultimately as a talking clown. Addressing politics, Rice became possibly the most well-known man in the country by 1860 and then ran for office from the circus ring, his legitimate campaigns including a brief bid for president. Famous for hilarity in both city and

country, North and South, in circus tents and on the nation's leading stages, he enlarged his already great fame by pitching refinement.
Matching the ideals (and costume) of the emerging middle class, he
began to perform in evening clothes and declared he was a sophisticated
artist "aspiring to something higher." Presenting himself as "The Great
American Humorist," he anticipated Twain, billed a generation later in
his own lecture tours as "The American Humorist." Meanwhile, Rice
periodically appeared as the "Shaksperian Jester." For many, "perhaps
the most amusing feature in his performance is his truly laughable burlesque readings of Shakspeare" (spelling of Shakespeare's name had not
yet become standardized).[8]

He may have first visited young Sam Clemens's hometown of Hannibal, Missouri, in 1844. Rice had been performing feats of strength
and comic songs upriver as a solo act in Davenport, Iowa, and the sim-
plest route back east would have taken him down the Mississippi past
Hannibal, to St. Louis and then Cairo, where the Ohio River branches
northeast. (That is the turn Huck and Jim miss on their raft, sending
them deeper into slave territory.) Rice would have looked for any opportunity to perform. "The show must go on" was not romance about
performers' pluck but cold, financial reality: no performance meant no
money. So Hannibal, with St. Louis another 150 miles downriver, would
have beckoned Rice as a likely spot to pick up some "rhino"—slang for
cash, as used by Twain in *Roughing It*. (The rhinoceros, including
Rice's, the first trained one since ancient Rome, was still known by the
full word.)[9]

Four years later Rice brought a circus to town. Although sleepy Hannibal could be called a backwater, that was never technically accurate,
as America's largest river sweeps mightily past. Nor was it even wholly
accurate as a symbol in 1848, for the Mississippi in the nineteenth century was one of the nation's major thoroughfares, plied by a constant
parade of commerce, travelers, and performers. The various adventures
Twain gave Huck and Jim reflect that busy fact. Soon, that north-south
traffic would multiply with easterners heading west on the California
Gold Rush in 1849. The city bias that cities exemplify sophisticated dis-
cernment falters next to the twin facts of occasional rural sophistication
and routine urban coarseness (not excluding the coarse understanding
of those whose mental horizon stops at city limits). That was especially
true in the nineteenth century, when cities were less dominant, and
many leading performers toured, allowing river towns to see the same
thing enjoyed in city theatres. So Rice would not have simplified for
Hannibal what he presented in New Orleans or New York. An astute

and sensitive performer, he would have adjusted to a different audience; he would not automatically have assumed a duller one.[10]

At the end of May 1848 the twenty-five-year-old talking clown steamed out of St. Louis on the *Allegheny Mail* with his "Dan Rice" circus, the first of many that would bear his name. He steered past Hannibal to Galena, in northern Illinois, before turning around to play towns on the way down. On June 26 he hauled up in Hannibal, bringing his horses, acrobats, and clowns, his sawdust ring and bleacher seats. He also brought Shakespeare.

He arrived to—and thirteen-year-old Sam Clemens certainly read— one of the most entertaining attacks the clown encountered in a half century of performing. Circuses were sporadically criticized because they were widely popular institutions that did not always meet the standards of self-appointed moralists. Rice's already strong popularity made him an especially prominent target. Although most observers praised his "Shaksperiana," there were exceptions. The editor of the *Hannibal Journal* was one. He called Rice's troupe a "motley gang of bacchanalian mountebanks" and its show "one of the most contemptibly obscene things . . . that has ever disgraced our city." He then turned his wrath on the leader:

> As to Dan Rice, the "great Shakspearian clown," we think the title Shakspearian *blackguard* would suit him much better. He is as perfectly devoid of true wit as he is of the principles of common decency, and every attempt he makes at anything of the kind is a mere slang drawling of the most repulsive obscenity. It is perfectly sickening to hear the most beautiful language and sublime ideas of the immortal "Bard of Avon" prostituted and mingled up with the most common place dram-shop slang by the sacriligious [*sic*] tongue of this brazen faced traducer who, leper like, turns every thing he touches to moral filth and uncleanliness.

Again, this harangue, however juicy, was a minority opinion. (Sam's brother, Orion Clemens, would take over as editor three years later.) Indeed, the rustic scribe's bile bubbled so high *because* other newspapers approved, as he flailed about the "noise . . . made by some of the presses of our neighboring cities." A few years later that "noise" would include the rival *Hannibal Tri-Weekly Messenger*, which declared of Rice that "a more modest clown never convulsed his audiences with laughter." The *Journal* spluttered in conclusion: "And yet, strange to tell, this misnomer of a circus, pandering as it does to some of the vilest passions of the human heart, is tolerated, nay, even largely encouraged by people who under other circumstances arrogate to themselves the title of a moral and even religious community."[11]

The fury must have been partly preemptive, the Hannibal editor bracing himself against the counterattack that was sure to come, as Rice was already noted for using the forum of the circus ring to thunder back at critics. Historians necessarily rely on nineteenth-century newspaper accounts, so it is easy to forget how much newspapers struggled to match the clout of speakers in that triumphantly oral age. The spoken word dominated public life, with few people reading any individual newspaper, yet only assiduous research and careful reading between the (written) lines can recover the spoken contribution to the rowdy public forum of antebellum life, and then only partly. Twain's rise resulted in large measure from his skill at transforming the orality of his boyhood into the written word for an increasingly literate and less-oral age. That earlier power in orality was especially true with the pugnacious populist Rice, who had a booming voice, a winning humor, and a nearly universal popularity that combined to give him a reach overwhelming that of nearly all antebellum papers. Horace Greeley's *New York Tribune* has come down through history as one of America's most significant newspapers, yet when Rice feuded with Greeley and his *Tribune*, it was considered an even contest. The *New York Clipper* commented on their "game of public give-and-take. The *Tribune* has a large circulation [but] Dan Rice, with a large audience, has been known to wield a tremendous influence. . . . For our part, we are generally advocates of peace; but in this case we don't care how long the fight lasts. It is a free fight. The pair are well matched." (Late in life, Rice must have relished clipping this tribute from the *Tribune*, his old nemesis: "As there never was but one Shakespeare, so there never will be but one Dan Rice.")[12] Rice's presence would have been tremendous in 1848 Hannibal.

Did young Clemens watch Rice's "Hamlet"? There is no direct evidence, yet it seems likely. Twain scholars assume that he attended Rice's circus as a boy, and they identify Rice's show as the model for the circus glowingly described in *Huckleberry Finn*. Blair and Fischer specifically mention the influence of Rice's "comic use of Shakespeare" on Twain. That influence should not be surprising. Circuses were one of the few bright spots in the daily monotony of rural America. As another Twain biographer, Dixon Wecter, wrote, "[T]he circus had seemed a passport to paradise. All the river towns had their barns plastered with the bills of yesterday's and tomorrow's troupe. The taprooms of every tavern were covered with the garish chromos, often running up the walls and continued above." Nearly everyone attended when a circus came to town. That would be particularly true when it was the renowned Dan

Rice and particularly true of sparks like Sam Clemens, who then and in his life as Mark Twain enjoyed amusements of all kinds. Just before leaving Hannibal behind, Sam inserted a plug for Rice's circus in his brother's paper. A literary influence would become available the year after Rice's first circus in Hannibal: his early ventures as mesmerist, actor, preacher, and the like appeared in *Sketches from the Life of Dan Rice, the Shakspearian Jester and Original Clown,* an 1849 press-agent embellishment that the boy Sam Clemens could have bought and devoured. Rice's arrival always generated excitement, and the tempest brewed by the *Hannibal Journal* would have made his visit in 1848 even more compelling. Most of the town would have turned out to hear Rice's response, and it is implausible that a spirited boy like Clemens would have missed it.[13]

What was the "Shaksperiana" Hannibal heard? Again, spoken words fade easily. Newspapers in various cities noted Rice's "Hamlet," without relating the words he used. The *St. Louis Daily Reveille* praised it specifically on May 16, 1848, before he embarked on the summer tour that would take him to Hannibal but, like its counterparts, included no excerpt. Not even the *Hannibal Journal* paused in its flailing to provide details of Rice's supposed "moral filth." Fortunately, a decade later he provided his own examples in a songster, *Dan Rice's Original Comic and Sentimental Poetic Effusions.* Songsters were pocket-sized pamphlets for sale, with lyrics of a clown's songs set to popular tunes. Rice set a few of his lyrics to music by his pal, from his early Pittsburgh days, Stephen Foster. Not surprisingly, Rice's *Poetic Effusions* included Shakespeare. They came in the form of two parodies, of *Othello* and *Hamlet.* Rice wrote neither one, but people knew them as his, just as singers have signature songs written by others. (For instance, Bob Hope, the twentieth-century counterpart to Rice's nineteenth-century reach, did not write his theme song, "Thanks for the Memories.")

"Dan Rice's Version of Othello" was featured on the songster's first page. It gives a complete synopsis of the original in seventy-two lines, like a Cliff's Notes version in rhymed couplets. In this one the comedy is muted, coming in a few antic couplets and occasional breezy vernacular, presumably the "dram-shop slang" that so shocked the Hannibal editor. Iago, for instance, was a "swiper" who got Cassio "drunk as any piper." The other parody, "Dan Rice's Multifarious Account of Shakespeare's Hamlet," is longer, at 104 lines, and more markedly comedic:

Hamlet, the Dane, of him just deign to hear,
And for that object lend at least one ear,
I will a tale unfold, whose lightest word

Will freeze your soul and turn your blood to curd.
      . . .
One night, two fellows, standing at their post,
Beheld, my stars! a real living ghost!
Whose ghost was he, so dismal and unhappy?
It was, my eyes! The ghost of Hamlet's pappy.
      . . .
And wasn't he mad to hear his daddy say
How Hamlet's uncle poisoned him one day,
As in his orchard he did take a snooze—
Well Hamlet was astonished at the news,
And swore by jingo, with prodigious rant,
To kill his uncle, pa and mother, aunt;
      . . .
      . . . and so they all did die,
Which is so dismal that it makes me cry—
Hububaluh-boo-boo-boo-a first-rate story
Some die for love, some they die for glory.

Despite the comic tone, this is not mere burlesque. It gives a complete account of the play, in regular iambic pentameter. (Teachers could do worse than this abridged version to introduce students to the play.) The last line's rhythm is awkward—"Some DIE for LOVE, some THEY die FOR glo-REE"—but as an exception, it must have been a concluding comic touch, what clowns now call a "blow-off." Again, audiences knew Shakespeare's poetic line from long experience, and would have gotten the joke.[14]

That sophistication included knowledge of actors. "Rice's Multifarious Account" relied on that awareness to incorporate performance commentary. Rice mocked excessive acting by playing off the florid pronunciation of the noted English actor Charles Kean, in this instance, Kean's rendering of *dew* spoken with an elaborate *d*:

He wanted his too solid flesh to melt,
Thaw, and resolve itself into a "jew" — / dew
Is the word, but Charley Keen says "jew,"
And I, the clown Shakspearean, say so too,
I wish I was tragedian, yes I do
I'd make about ye'r ears the worst of clatters,
And tear my shirt and passion into tatters.

Turning to the play-within-a-play of the original, Rice's "Hamlet" touched on a bit of stage business destined soon to become historically significant:

So he got up a play—they played so bad,
It made the king and courtiers dreadful mad;
Gracious, how he did fly around and prance—
Just in this place Macready makes him dance—[15]

This refers to a routine the British star William Macready interpolated into his productions of *Hamlet,* dancing around and waving a handkerchief to signal the prince's madness. That led to the most important hiss in American theatre history. In 1846 the American star Edwin Forrest crossed the Atlantic for a tour and went to watch his rival perform Hamlet in Edinburgh, Scotland. Theatre histories usually depict Forrest as the physical counterpart to Macready's presumed intellectual, researching his parts, but Forrest was just as serious about his own Shakespearean scholarship, and it convinced him that this little handkerchief dance was a blot on the play. He may have equated it with the ditties common in Shakespeare parodies, like "Oh, dear, what can the matter be" in John Poole's *Hamlet Travestie.* Or Forrest could have seen it as emblematic of his rival's excessive style: the comedian Dan Marble, joking about the handkerchief dance—a "*pas de muchoir*"—considered it part of Macready's "pile-up-the-agony-talent."[16] Of course, jealousy cannot be discounted, the rising star growling at the fading one. Whatever the reason, Forrest hissed. Hissing—no one booed yet—was the accepted method of expressing displeasure from the seats, a nineteenth-century version of a critic's review. Nevertheless, Macready took offense, and their simmering rivalry boiled into a feud. When the two actors presented dueling Macbeths at different New York theatres in the spring of 1849, their respective supporters bubbled until the feud exploded into a riot, killing dozens. The Astor Place Riot stands as America's biggest theatre riot. Yet even before the notoriety of the riot highlighted the feud and its details, Rice's "Multifarious Hamlet" referred to Macready's dance without explanation. Audiences would have known about it and gotten the joke.

Traditional historiography has shoved the nuances of the era's performance into conveniently opposed categories. Taking the side of Macready's supporters and his publicity, it poses his presumed restraint against a crude Forrest, reducing the American to one trait, physicality, or two, adding "rant." (Historians find that bifurcation convenient, obscuring the fact that Thomas Hamblin presented a *third* Macbeth in New York that May.) So it is ironic that their feud was sparked by the Brit's physicality, and a crude bit at that. Pushing irony further, the public posture of the circus clown Rice and the "intellectual" Macready matched. A few months before the riot, a Macready partisan explicitly yoked them together:

> Dan belongs to a new race, not the clown of the stage, the pantomime, nor even the ring, but the pure American clown—in fact, you may call him the Macready of the circle, he is a profoundly intellectual and scholar like specimen of a clown. Instead of relying upon the somersaults and tricks of his predecessors, he strikes into a quieter, anti-physical, school of performance—indeed he is the reading, not acting edition of the clown.[17]

By the 1880s Rice's reputation had fallen. His "quieter, anti-physical, school of performance" had helped create the idea that "higher" performance—increasingly called "art"—required such sophistication. Playing to huge crowds, city and country, North and South, "The Great American Humorist" who "aspired to something higher" had a prominent role in that cultural shift. Nevertheless, the "Shakespeare clown" sank to an oxymoron, culturally inexplicable except as a joke, clownishness overwhelming Shakespearean sophistication, the low swamping the high, levity conquering gravity. Meanwhile, Shakespeare's reputation rose to new heights as the epitome of refined sophistication. Along with once merely popular forms like opera and ballet, the Bard of Avon became the standard against which other kinds of performance were judged, and he was usually found wanting. Rice, even in his decline, stayed attuned to the evolving culture and so fit himself to the new expectations of the clown as a tedious buffoon. Rice claimed that his use of Shakespeare went no further than simple burlesque of Macbeth's "Is this a dagger I see before me?" Rice said he twisted it to doggerel:

> Is that a beefsteak I see before me
> With the burnt side toward my hand?
> Let me clutch thee! I have thee not,
> And yet I see thee still in form as palpable
> As that I ate for breakfast this morning.

But this self-mockery, which apparently did not find its way into print until after his death, ignored that he had flourished using Shakespeare well. The *Cincinnati Commercial Gazette* ignored it, too, in 1883, using Shakespeare as the counterexample. Declaring that the talking clown's time was past, "the silent clown now usurping his place," the newspaper retrospectively pictured Rice as an instinctive but ignorant fool, parading through the streets in a coach "with a handsomely bound copy of the great William's works open before him, when, had his life depended upon it, he could not have spelled out a single word of the text." It was the same kind of retrospective fiction Twain would soon peddle in *Huckleberry Finn*—in his own attempt to scale highbrow heights—of antebellum performance as paltry stuff.[18]

Pronouncing *Huckleberry Finn* great, Lionel Trilling declared that its excellence lies "[p]rimarily in its power of telling the truth."[19] Part of that presumed truth was the image Twain crafted of bad performers and dim-witted audiences. Yet Twain's "Hamlet's Soliloquy" is false in its implication of a benighted past succeeded by a progressive present. Instead, it shows an accomplished writer in the 1880s fitting himself to the new conventional wisdom, flattering his readers in their would-be elevation. Trilling's "truth" can be more nearly approached in this great book by giving antebellum performance more credit than historiographic tradition allows. Reverse the picture. Ignore the cultural and ahistorical bias that deems antebellum performers paltry and audiences stupid—a bias fostered by "The Great American Humorist" Rice and then "The American Humorist" Twain. Instead consider Twain's "Shaksperiana" as if it were a clue in a detective story, the truth hidden in plain sight. Pretend you are the audience, which presumably means you consider the audience an intelligent one, and assume that those rigorously experienced performers had a wide range of skills, including deadpan, silence, and subtlety. Imagine settling back to listen to a nineteenth-century Robin Williams, sharp, experienced, hilarious. He enters the arena, pauses, looks grave, and then intones, "To be or not to be; that is the bare bodkin / That makes calamity of so long life," before swinging to "And makes us rather sling the arrows of outrageous fortune / Than fly to others that we know not of." Done well, that becomes a funny moment shared by an astute performer and a knowing audience. Just as Rice shared hilarity with his audiences, presumably including Twain-to-be Sam Clemens. Stripped of encrusted interpretation, this "Hamlet's Soliloquy" begins to sound less like a parody of ludicrous rustics and more like a gloss on—or copy of—performances Twain had enjoyed. Like a transcript of an unearthed nineteenth-century Shakespearean performance. Like Rice's "Hamlet."

The boisterously oral clown concluded his "Othello" with a couplet boasting that his verse excelled Shakespeare's. That boast was an ironic joke, enjoyed by his own age. Dan Rice can also be envisioned using it without irony, comparing himself to others who employed the Bard's verse, actors then and writers to come, as he said: "This tale is writ in Shakespeare's lyric finis / But his account is not as good as mine is."

Notes

1. Twain also toyed with an extended *Hamlet* parody but gave it up. See Franklin P. Rogers, ed., *Mark Twain's Satires and Burlesques* (Berkeley: University of California Press, 1967), 49–87.

2. Andrew Hoffman, *Inventing Mark Twain: The Lives of Samuel Langhorne Clemens* (New York: William Morrow, 1997), xiii.

3. I have dealt elsewhere with two of these historiographic problems. The apparently trite endings of melodramas are usually characterized as a weakness, but such assessments substitute twenty-first-century notions for the dynamics of nineteenth-century performance, framed but not limited by its conventions (see David Carlyon, "The Radical Promise of Melodrama's Happy Endings" [paper presented at the Association for Theatre in Higher Education (ATHE) conference, Chicago, July 1994]). As for the rustics who do not know they are watching a show, the alleged instances, recycled from history to history, turn out to be mostly fiction, again founded less on evidence than cultural bias that marginalized rubes, blacks, Indians, Mormons, and women then and nineteenth-century audiences now (see David Carlyon, "'Blow your nose with your fingers': The Rube Story as Crowd Control," *New England Theatre Journal* 7 [1996]: 1–22).

4. Walter Kerr made the point half a century ago in his *How Not to Write a Play* (New York: Simon & Schuster, 1955). For an international flavor see Jim Davis and Victor Emeljanow, *Reflecting the Audience: London Theatregoing, 1840–1880* (Iowa City: University of Iowa Press, 2001); and James H. Johnson, *Listening in Paris: A Cultural History* (Berkeley: University of California Press, 1995).

5. Lawrence Levine, *Highbrow/Lowbrow: The Emergence of a Cultural Hierarchy* (Cambridge, MA: Harvard University Press, 1988).

6. Raymond Williams, *Culture and Society: 1780–1950* (New York: Harper, 1966), xv–xvi. The absence of "art" or "entertainment" in news of "the show business" before the 1850s supports Williams's point; it was all "amusements" then.

7. Walter Blair and Victor Fischer, eds., *The Works of Mark Twain*, vol. 8, *The Adventures of Huckleberry Finn* (Berkeley: University of California Press, 1988), 411; George A. Speaight, "A Note on Shakespearean Clowns," *Nineteenth Century Theatre Research* 7, no. 2 (autumn 1979): 93–98. Also see Jonathan Bate, "Parodies of Shakespeare," *Journal of Popular Culture* 19, no. 1 (summer 1985): 75–90; Claudia D. Johnson, "Burlesques of Shakespeare: The Democratic American's 'Light Artillery,'" *Theatre Survey* 21 (May 1980): 49–62; James Ellis, "The Counterfeit Presentment: Nineteenth-Century Burlesques of *Hamlet*," *Nineteenth Century Theatre Research* 11, no. 1 (summer 1983): 29–50; A. H. Saxon, "Shakespeare and Circuses," *Theatre Survey* 7, no. 2 (Nov. 1966): 59–79.

8. David Carlyon, *Dan Rice: The Most Famous Man You've Never Heard Of* (New York: Public Affairs, 2001); *Baltimore Sun*, Apr. 11, 1846.

9. *Davenport Gazette*, Mar. 28, 1844; Council Minutes, City of Davenport, Iowa, Mar. 30, 1844, 112; Mark Twain, *Roughing It* (Hartford, CT: American, 1872), 387.

10. Hoffman, *Inventing Mark Twain*, 25.

11. *Hannibal Journal*, June 26, 1848; *Hannibal Tri-Weekly Messenger*, Aug. 24, 1852.

12. *New York Clipper*, Feb. 19, 1859, 350; *New York Tribune*, n.d., loose clipping, dark blue scrapbook, compiled by Rice, author's collection.

13. Blair and Fischer, *Works*, 8:411; Dixon Wecter, *Sam Clemens of Hannibal* (Boston: Houghton-Mifflin, 1952), 191–92; [Wessel T. B. Van Orden], *Sketches from the Life of Dan Rice, the Shakspearian Jester and Original Clown* (Albany, NY, 1849).

14. *Dan Rice's Original Comic and Sentimental Poetic Effusions* (New Orleans, 1859), 1, 14. Rice apparently got his "Othello" from the amusement weekly *Spirit of the Times*, May 8, 1841, 120, quoting *Dublin University Magazine*. Twain could also have read a *Hamlet* pastiche in an actress's memoirs: Olive Logan, *Before the Footlights and behind the Scenes* (Philadelphia, 1870), 405. Logan's insistence that she sought to rise above her profession's vulgar reputation would have commended itself to Twain, who was struggling to rise above a similar reputation.

15. Rice, *Effusions.*

16. John Poole, *Hamlet Travestie* (1810), London, 1816, 36; Falconbridge [pseud.], *Dan Marble: A Biographical Sketch*, New York, [ca. 1851], 75.

17. *Spirit of the Times*, Feb. 10, 1849, 612.

18. Maria Ward Brown, *The Life of Dan Rice* (Long Branch, NJ: Author, 1901), 172; *Cincinnati Commercial Gazette*, June 3, 1883.

19. Lionel Trilling, *The Liberal Imagination* (New York: Viking, 1950), 105.

Are You Shakespearienced?

Rock Music and Contemporary
American Production of Shakespeare

Kevin J. Wetmore Jr.

"Hair, Prince of Denmark":
Rock-and-Roll Shakespeare, an Introduction

In 1966 Gerome Ragni and James Rado teamed up with a composer named Galt MacDermot. MacDermot had composed some songs for a few revues in Montreal, but his work with the two young actors, a "free-form musical" entitled *Hair*, designed to transform theatre and provide a new model for musicals, was his first full-length effort. *Hair*, called "The American Tribal Love Rock Musical" by its creators, was one of the first American musicals to use rock and roll as its dominant musical style.[1] It was also one of the first plays to combine an Americanized Shakespeare with rock and roll.

The play tells the story of Claude Hooper Bukowski, a hippie who has been drafted to go to Vietnam, and his friends Berger, Hud, Woof, Crissy, Sheila, and "the Tribe."[2] The first version of the play featured Berger and Claude speaking Hamlet's "What a piece of work is man!" speech as a dialogue. In later versions the speech became a song.

In the Broadway production the cast sang "Three-Five-Zero-Zero," an antiwar song, after the stage was littered with the bodies of dead soldiers and dead Native Americans from historic wars. Two cast members then walked among the dead bodies singing "What a Piece of Work

Is Man," a song that slightly alters the original text. Rado and Ragni begin the song with act 2, scene 2, line 303, "What a piece of work is man . . . ," and continue through line 307, "the paragon of animals." The song then returns to an earlier point in the speech, editing the text for rhythm and rhyme:

> I have of late—but wherefore I know not—lost all my mirth.
> This goodly frame the earth seems to me a sterile promontory;
> this most excellent canopy, the air, look you;
> this brave o'erhanging firmament, this majestical roof fretted with
> golden fire, why it appears no other thing to me than a foul and
>   pestilent
> congregation of vapors. (2.2.295–96, 298–303)

The piece then concludes by repeating the first two lines now in the original place: "What a piece of work is man, how noble in reason." The authors intend, as Hamlet did, for the words to be taken ironically— for, "to me what is this quintessence of dust? Man delights not me" (2.2.308–9). Whereas Hamlet is disgusted with what is rotten in the state of Denmark, the authors of *Hair* use Shakespeare's words to decry what is rotten in the state of America in the Vietnam War era.

At the conclusion of the musical Claude has passed his medical exam, been sent to basic training, and then to Vietnam, where he is killed. At his death Claude sang a song called "Eyes Look Your Last," taken directly from Romeo's death speech in *Romeo and Juliet* (5.3.112).[3] Claude's last song, "The Flesh Failures," features a chorus that sings after he dies, following his last lines with a repetition of the phrases "Seal with a righteous kiss" (*Romeo and Juliet* 5.3.114—taken from the same speech as the previous reference) and "The rest is silence" (*Hamlet* 5.2.358), the final words of Romeo and Hamlet.

Ragni and Rado sought not to create a rock-and-roll Shakespeare but rather to use familiar lines from the plays to link their tragic young heroes with Shakespeare's. Hamlet and Romeo are, apart from Troilus, Shakespeare's only youthful tragic male protagonists. They both die because of conflicts with the older generation. *Hair* places Claude into the same tragic model—a young man born "to set things right," who, only desiring to love and live free, dies in a conflict not of his own making, a fight between members of the older generation. In the 1960s in the United States, Hamlet and Romeo had become figures of youthful rebellion, and the music of youthful rebellion was rock and roll. Shakespeare's plays do not have to be presented in their entirety, using the original texts, the experiment seemed to say, but rather can serve as intertexts, mixed with rock-and-roll music to develop theatre for a younger generation.

In this essay I consider the mutual expropriation of Shakespeare and rock and roll in American production. Rock-music-centered adaptations of Shakespeare not only appropriate the texts of the plays (in fact, in some cases the text is not appropriated at all, but erased!), but they also exploit and explore what "Shakespeare" represents. In other words they explore the idea of "Shakespeare," not just as a playwright but as a cultural phenomenon occupying a singular place in American culture. I argue that such productions adapt the concept of Shakespeare as much as the actual texts for the paradoxical purposes of both legitimizing contemporary alternative performance through the use of alleged "high" culture and creating an accessible, demystified Shakespeare for contemporary audiences through familiar cultural referents. This use of Shakespeare's plays begs the larger question of what is "Shakespearean" about Shakespeare, which is also considered below. Finally, I contextualize such productions as adaptations, rock musicals, and a return to earlier constructions of "American Shakespeare."

Hair was produced by Joseph Papp, the creator of Shakespeare in Central Park. In 1969 Papp commissioned Galt MacDermot to write the rock score for his *William Shakespeare's "Naked" Hamlet*, staged at the Public Theatre in New York. The production, starring a young Martin Sheen, was a collage of the original text, designed to deconstruct audience assumptions about Shakespeare and his most famous play.

The production handbook begins by noting a series of actions designed to prompt "guesses" by the audience as to what the production might be. "The Third Guess" consists of "a minute of rock music" designed to make the audience ask, "Is this going to be a rock *Hamlet*? . . . And what is a rock *Hamlet* anyway?"[4] In scene 30 all of Ophelia's songs are performed at once, as a "vaudeville/rock show," with original rock music by MacDermot. Papp claims that the music grew organically out of the company's exploration of the text: "We found . . . rock music in the play, so we put [it] in the production."[5]

The production was loudly decried by many critics and many older audience members. The *New York Times* critic referred to the production as "a *Hamlet* for the Philistines."[6] Yet, as Joseph Papp observes in his preface to the production handbook, "the Public Theatre was jammed every night" with an audience mostly in their teens and twenties.[7] The loud rock music and the deconstructive nature of the production, which rearranged Shakespeare's text and added new elements, such as Hamlet disguising himself as "Ramon the Puerto Rican Janitor," demonstrated that the target audience was not one that favored traditional readings of the text or standard (for the time) interpretations of its meaning.[8] Everything about the play was loud and rebellious, arguably the very qualities that define rock and roll.

We should note that both Papp and MacDermot continued blending Shakespeare and rock and roll. Papp used rock music in numerous productions for Shakespeare in Central Park. In 1973 MacDermot teamed up with John Guare and Mel Shapiro to create a rock-and-roll version of *The Two Gentlemen of Verona.*[9]

Shakespeare's works were linked to rock and roll in a variety of manners. In the same year Papp presented his rock-and-roll *Hamlet*, Tony Richardson cast Marianne Faithful, famed groupie and rock artist in her own right, as Ophelia in his *Hamlet.* The same year that MacDermot rocked Verona, Patrick McGoohan directed *Catch My Soul*, a rock opera adaptation of *Othello.* The BBC, when creating its complete works of Shakespeare on video, cast The Who's Roger Daltry as Dromio in *The Comedy of Errors.* Very quickly Shakespeare's plays came to occupy the same cultural space as rock-and-roll music through the expropriation of Shakespeare (the man and the plays, characters, and words) by rock music and through the use of rock music in American productions of Shakespeare.

American Rock and Roll Expropriates Shakespeare

If rock and roll has shaped production and reception of Shakespeare, it is only fair to observe that Shakespeare has also shaped rock and roll, at least the lyrical content. In particular, Shakespeare's Romeo and Juliet are perhaps the bard's greatest contributions to rock and roll. If, as Paul Friedlander argues, "the dominant topic in rock music lyrics has always been romance," then Romeo and Juliet, as the archetypical romantic couple, have served as the ultimate rock-and-roll reference for young love.[10]

Stephen Buhler has thoroughly documented the transformations of Romeo and Juliet in pop music and cataloged their presence in pop lyrics.[11] A random, and far from complete, sampling would include "(Just like) Romeo and Juliet," by The Reflections (1964); "(Don't Fear) the Reaper," by Blue Oyster Cult (1976); "Romeo Is Bleeding," by Tom Waits (1978); "Romeo and Juliet," by Dire Straits (1980); "Romeo Had Juliette," by Lou Reed (1989); three direct references by Bruce Springsteen alone (in "Incident on 54th Street" in 1973, "Fire" in 1979, and "Point Blank" in 1980); and songs by Ratt, Alanis Morissette, Aerosmith, Madonna, Kool and the Gang, Elvis Costello, Michael

Penn, Bob Dylan, and the Indigo Girls. Romeo and Juliet are referenced in rock lyrics hundreds of times more than the next-most-popular Shakespeare character, Ophelia, who has been mentioned in songs by such artists as the Indigo Girls and Natalie Merchant (both of whom have also invoked Polonius's much-put-upon daughter in album titles, *Swamp Ophelia* [1994] and *Ophelia* [1998], respectively) and in the names of such bands as San Francisco–based The Ophelias and Boston-based Ophelia Rising.[12]

Pop music Romeo and Juliet references, however, reinscribe not Shakespeare's play but the characters themselves as pop culture celebrities, leaving them with more in common with "Bogey and Bacall" (Bertie Higgins, "Key Largo," 1981), Bette Davis and her eyes (Kim Carnes, 1981), Captain Jean-Luc Picard of the United Federation of Planets (Refreshments, "Bandito," 1997), or, perhaps most accurately, Superman (take your pick: The Kinks, Donovan, R. E. M., Roy Gaines, Eminem, Three Doors Down, Spin Doctors, Five for Fighting, The Flaming Lips, and the Ominous Seapods, among others) than with the characters of Shakespeare's plays.[13] As a result, it is not Shakespeare's play that is being referenced but the idea of romantic love as embodied in the characters, and they are the equivalents of any other pop-culture figures— real or fictional. One need not be familiar with Shakespeare's play—only the idea (or ideal) of the characters.

In much the same way, Shakespeare the man—or perhaps more accurately, Shakespeare the concept—lent his name to rock and roll in the 1980s. Robbie Shakespeare, the well-known reggae producer and bass player, took his name from the swan of Avon. In the mid-1980s Minneapolis-based "Trip Shakespeare" formed, titling their second album "Are You Shakespearienced?," a play on Jimi Hendrix's "Are You Experienced." Forming in 1989, "Shakespeare's Sister," consisting of Siobhan Fahey and Marcella Detroit, released two albums before breaking up. Although not well known in the United States, they achieved great popularity in Europe and England. The name "Shakespeare" is synonymous in American society with high culture, British cultural superiority, "drama," and great writing. Bands that employ his name in theirs seek to define themselves, sometimes ironically, in terms of Shakespeare.

The name "William Shakespeare" is used not only by bands but by directors who seek to shape the plays but retain a sense of authority and authenticity, in much the same way that rock musicians seek through the use of the name to establish their own artistic skills and authenticity. Papp's titling his production *William Shakespeare's "Naked" Hamlet* serves the same purpose as Baz Luhrmann's titling his film *William*

Shakespeare's Romeo and Juliet nearly three decades later.[14] In both cases the product was aimed at a youth market, and Shakespeare's name was placed in front not only in order to assert the primacy of the author but to buttress the new work by ascribing it to Shakespeare, giving the work a gloss of authenticity that the textual and visual deconstructions of Papp and Luhrmann do not always have.

Lynda E. Boose and Richard Burt note in their introduction to *Shakespeare: The Movie* that "youth culture" by and large dominates the milieu of most current films based on Shakespeare (vis-à-vis *O, Ten Things I Hate about You, William Shakespeare's Romeo and Juliet, Clueless,* among others) and that "major Shakespearean critics are turning their talents to the reading of MTV videos."[15] The largest (at least in terms of attention given by the media) of these is Luhrmann's film, which many critics believed was as much rooted in rock culture as it was in Shakespeare.[16] Not one but two sound-track CDs were issued.[17] MTV did a half-hour special on Baz Luhrmann's *William Shakespeare's Romeo and Juliet,* further linking that film to the world of rock and roll. One critic complained the film was "more concerned with its rock/hip-hop sound-track than with any Shakespearean verse."[18] Yet James Loehlin sees the rock sound track as being "sonic flair," which is used to "balance out the weaknesses in the film, notably the vocal shortcomings of the cast."[19]

Where teen heartthrobs Leonardo DiCaprio and Clare Danes fail to do Shakespeare's verse justice, One Inch Punch, the Butthole Surfers, and Stina Nordenstam support the text by referencing it in the music and, arguably, offer a more poetic interpretation of some of the lines. Many of the songs on the sound track echo lines from *Romeo and Juliet,* placing Shakespeare's text into a rock context. For example, almost all of the lyrics from "Pretty Piece of Flesh," by One Inch Punch, come from the opening scene between the servants of the two households:

I strike quickly being moved (1.1.5)
The weakest goes to the wall (1.1.12)
I am a pretty piece of flesh (1.1.28)

Similarly, lines from the play occur in "Local God," by Everclear; "To You I Bestow," by Mundy; and "Whatever," by the Butthole Surfers— all contemporary American alternative rock bands invited to contribute to the sound track. For Luhrmann it was not enough to have rock music in the Shakespearean film; it was necessary to have Shakespearean verse in the rock sound track.[20]

Mary Lindroth takes this argument even further by stating that the sound track of Luhrmann's film serves the same purpose in the movie that music did in Shakespeare's play: to entertain the audience, to "shape the audience's experience," "to signal a change in scene, a change in tone, [or] a change in pace," and works with the camera to tell the story.[21] In other words, just as the music in Shakespeare's original production served a variety of purposes, but was inarguably "contemporary music," Luhrmann's film uses contemporary music of the present (rock and "pop") to serve the same purposes in his film version. Luhrmann, clearly directing for a youth audience, relies on a heavily edited text, a strong popular-music sound track, and, in Loehlin's words, "MTV-style camera work and editing" to recreate Shakespeare's play for generations X and Y.[22] *William Shakespeare's Romeo and Juliet* is the most obvious example but neither the first nor last film to cinematize Shakespeare for the alternative pop and hip-hop generations.[23]

Expropriation of Rock Songs in American Productions of Shakespeare

If productions of Shakespeare in the 1960s used rock to rebel, productions in the 1980s, 1990s, and the current decade have used rock nostalgically. This fact may be partly attributable to the aging of the baby-boom generation, who were in their teens and early twenties in the 1960s, and to the trend to commercialization in contemporary rock music. As Dennis Hopper has stated, "The counterculture has become the culture."[24]

In every period since the Elizabethan the production of Shakespeare's plays has expropriated contemporary music from the period. Shakespeare has always been "adapted" by using the popular music of the day, whether operatic adaptation, the addition of songs and/or dances, or incidental music. Nineteenth-century America saw burlesques, vaudevilles, and even minstrel show pastiches/adaptations of Shakespeare. The twentieth century saw numerous Broadway-style adaptations of Shakespeare's plays, renegotiating American cultural space through this indigenous dramatic form.[25]

Unlike earlier musical adaptations of Shakespeare, such as *Kiss Me Kate* and *The Boys from Syracuse*, which had original songs, and *Hair* and *"Naked" Hamlet*, which gave a rock sound track to Shakespeare's text, the new American Shakespearean adaptations use songs from popular music alongside Shakespeare's prose to develop new pieces or, perhaps more accurately, new pastiches, similar to the nineteenth-century variation. The first adaptation to do so was actually a British production based on *The Tempest*, entitled *Return to the Forbidden*

Planet. First performed in May of 1983 by the Bubble Theatre Company in England and revised and performed all over the world, with extended runs in London and New York, Bob Carlton's rock-and-roll musical blends Shakespearean text with the 1956 film *Forbidden Planet,* itself adapted from Shakespeare's *The Tempest.*[26] The play also uses sections of text from *Romeo and Juliet* and *A Midsummer Night's Dream* and incorporates 1950s and 1960s rock music to induce nostalgia, as well as to advance the plot: "Great Balls of Fire," by Jerry Lee Lewis; "Please Don't Let Me Be Misunderstood" and "We Gotta Get Out of This Place," by the Animals; "Why Must I Be a Teenager in Love?" by Frankie Lymon and the Teenagers; "Who's Sorry Now?" by Connie Francis; and Bobby "Boris" Pickett's "Monster Mash." The songs were not original to the show. The pleasure (and meaning) for the audience came from the use of a familiar song in a different context—in this case Shakespeare's play via a science fiction film.

The Troubadour Theatre Company of Los Angeles has taken the model of *Return to the Forbidden Planet* and created a style of adaptation and production from it. Blending contemporary clown and commedia dell'arte techniques with the philosophy of Brecht and the plays of Shakespeare, the "Troubies," as they call themselves, have deconstructed several of Shakespeare's plays through blending the narrative with the songs of a particular 1970s or 1980s rock group. These productions, including *Twelfth Dog Night, A Midsummer Saturday Night's Fever Dream, Romeo Hall and Juliet Oates, All's Kool That Ends Kool,* and, most recently (as of this writing), *Fleetwood Macbeth,* have been critical and popular successes for their reliance on double reference— familiarity with both Shakespeare and popular music—to tell their stories in an entertaining way. The improvisational and interactive sections of each show blend with the set pieces of Shakespeare and rock songs to create something not quite Shakespeare and yet wholly dependent on the plays and one's perception of them.[27]

The Troubadours were founded in 1993 and presented a pair of clown-based Shakespearean adaptations in the mid-1990s: *Clown's Labour's Lost,* a circus version of *Love's Labour's Lost;* and *Shrew!,* a clown *Taming of the Shrew.* Beginning in 1999, however, the company (through the lead of its artistic director, Matt Walker) began to blend 1970s rock and roll with Shakespearean texts. The first such production was *Twelfth Dog Night,* a blending of Shakespeare's *Twelfth Night* with the music of Three Dog Night.[28]

The program of the show states that the play was written by "the Company (with add'l material by William Shakespeare)," a humorous credit indicative of the company's focus: not on preserving the Shakespearean original but on reshaping the entire experience by the actors for the audience. We might also note that the Troubadours are based in Los Angeles, the same city that produced the infamous credit "By William Shakespeare, with additional dialogue by Sam Taylor," for the 1929 film version of *Taming of the Shrew* starring Douglas Fairbanks and Mary Pickford. The program credit may further be a parody of this famous attribution. After *Clown's Labour's Lost* and *Shrew!*, which were very loosely based on the originals, this production was, in the words of one reviewer, the "Troubadour's most faithful production of a Shakespeare play," although the reviewer does admit that "it still won't satisfy the purists."[29]

When Orsino, stating that "music be the food of love," asks the musicians to "play on," they perform "Just an Old-Fashioned Love Song." When Malvolio is locked up for being mad by Toby, Andrew, Feste, and Maria, he sings "One Is the Loneliest Number." Viola sings "Mama Told Me Not to Come" in response to Olivia's attempted seduction, and the whole company rejoices at the end with "Joy to the World."[30]

Over and above the musical additions, the actors metatheatrically engage the fact that they are performing not Shakespeare but a pastiche of Shakespeare. For example, at one point the characters, desiring to check the Shakespearean original to see how far away from it they have come, pull out not Shakespeare's text but the Cliff's Notes for the play. Nonsensical choices are commented on by the performers: Viola is played by an African American woman, and Sebastian is played by a Euro-American man, prompting the characters to ask why anyone is confusing the twins at all. Other popular-culture references abound, further removing the play from the realm of high culture. The reenactment of the shipwreck is accompanied by the theme from *Gilligan's Island*. In response to Malvolio's threats to his mistress's uncle and his friends, one of them remarks, "You look like a Klingon." The topical references of Shakespeare's day are replaced with contemporary topical references.

The consultation of the Cliff's Notes by the characters indicates that this particular type of "Shakespearean offshoot," to use Ruby Cohn's term, is not an attempt to replicate Shakespeare's original texts in new contexts. The Troubies' show is as much about the idea of Shakespeare and the popular cultural concept of Shakespeare as it is about the original text. Double reference is employed, but it is not even necessary to know the original—one need only know "Shakespeare." The productions are not concerned with authenticity of text, which raises questions of what is being "lost" in such adaptations and to what end, to what extent contemporary audiences have actual knowledge about Shakespeare, and what experiencing such productions teaches the audience (and the scholar) about Shakespeare and the Elizabethan theatre. Limitation of space does not allow me to explore such topics here, but they follow naturally from the issues raised.

Instead, I would like to focus on the idea that "rock-and-roll Shakespeare," whether practiced by the Troubies or by Baz Luhrmann, problematizes Shakespeare not only by adapting the texts of the plays, and linking nostalgic rock music to it, but also by adapting the idea or concept of "Shakespeare." In popular culture Shakespeare is often perceived as epitomizing "high culture," even though the very presence of Shakespeare in popular culture indicates a far more complex relationship linking the canon, the playwright, and popular, high, mass, and mass-produced culture—what Michael Bristol terms "Bardbiz." Shakespeare as cultural icon serves multiple functions in these productions.

First, Shakespeare as the embodiment of "high" culture can be invoked in production to grant legitimacy to performances and productions equally yoked to mass or popular culture. Rather than rock music serving Shakespeare, the "Shakespeare" in the piece serves the rock music. Second, as Shakespeare the concept is a distant and scary thing, served up in high school as part of education and "culture," he is "bad" and boring. In order to rescue the plays from this context, the rock-and-roll adapters attempt to demystify Shakespeare by making his plots, characters, and occasionally language accessible and not too distant from more contemporary entertainments. In other words, the rock music serves the Shakespearean text as a vehicle.

These contrasting uses of Shakespeare the concept raise the larger issue of what is "Shakespeare" about Shakespeare? The Troubies consult the Cliff's Notes rather than the actual text. They replace Shakespeare's poetry with more familiar rock songs. Shakespeare's plays are rooted in his language and poetry, yet that is precisely what many of the adaptations listed here remove and/or replace with rock music. What remains are Shakespeare's plots and characters, which were borrowed in the first place. When Shakespeare is expropriated through rock music (or rock music expropriated to serve Shakespeare) in American cultural space, more often than not what is being adapted is Shakespeare the concept as much as the play itself.

For example, in 2002 *All's Kool That Ends Kool* blended the plot of *All's Well . . .* with the funk music of Kool and the Gang.[31] Unlike in the previous three shows, the Troubies were attempting to produce a lesser-known play, leading one to ask what, precisely, is being decontextualized here: the Shakespearean play or the popular music? Arguably, both are being decontextualized. Again, Shakespeare's plotline stays intact, but well-known rock songs are introduced to the narrative. When the songs work, they really work, such as when the lords, Bertram, and Parolles prepare for Bertram's wooing of Diana by singing "Ladies Night," or when "Cherish" is sung ironically at the wedding of the unwilling Bertram and Helena in act 2, scene 3, or (the rather obvious) singing of "Celebration" at the conclusion of the play, when Bertram agrees to remain with Helena. Some of the song choices, however, seem arbitrary, such as when the company sings "Jungle Boogie" as Helena cures the king in act 2, scene 1. This production perhaps best showcases the strengths and weaknesses of the approach.

Perhaps the most telling moment in the production is when Bertram (played by artistic director Matt Walker) woos the widow and her daughter and actually uses the exact lines from the Shakespearean original. The lines flow and sound remarkably smooth, even as we recognize their heightened artifice. After a beat Walker turns to the audience and says, "That's what this is all supposed to sound like—pretty good stuff, huh?" Walker does not, however, drop character at that moment as he does at other times in the play, instead keeping his Bertram voice and demeanor. We become aware of the numerous levels of reference—a character aware that he is a character, not in a Shakespeare play but a play based on Shakespeare, and aware of the difference between the audience's Shakespearean expectations and Troubadour expectations. The fact that the performer delivers the original Shakespearean lines so well further blurs the reality of the show. The performers could perform Shakespeare as written, had they chosen to, says Walker, even as he acknowledges that the stuff is "pretty good." He also acknowledges that the original is how *All's Well* is "supposed to sound." But this production is not *All's Well*; it is *All's Kool*—the change in name connoting more than a change in text, indeed, a change in attitude.

The Troubadours are interested in appealing to all ages. The use of classical rock provokes nostalgia for the older members of the audience. The combination of clowning and rock music is to provide mediation for younger audience members. Walker claims, "If we can help them to become interested in Shakespeare at a young age, hopefully they will appreciate good theatre as adults."[32] The presumption behind Walker's remark is that the Troubadours' version of Shakespeare is not only "good theatre" but also an authentic Shakespeare in which young audience members might become interested. He may be right (his productions, after all, are always critical and popular successes), but any audience member who looks to the original text to see what was present in a Troubie production will find the two are remarkably different. What has been offered up onstage is an approximation of Shakespeare the concept as much as (if not more so than) an adaptation of the original play.

It is ironic and appropriate that the Troubadour productions are hailed as innovative, considering that they link two cultural pasts—the Elizabethan/Jacobean theatre and classic American rock and roll. These productions also reflect similar cultural trends—the predominance of music video in the last decades of the twentieth century and the first decade of the twenty-first means music has become more visually oriented, even as productions of Shakespeare move further away from text and more toward the visual. The Troubadours displace the text of Shakespeare with references to Shakespeare and create a new visual narrative for the popular song.

The Troubie productions are not so much adaptations as pastiches. They do not so much adapt Shakespeare as mediate between the text, the idea of "Shakespeare," and American popular culture. The rock music bridges the gaps of high and popular culture, old and modern, British and American. In their discussion of Shakespearean films of the 1990s Lynda E. Boose and Richard Burt observe that Shakespeare "is such a signifier for British cultural superiority."[33] Yet rock and roll is as American as the proverbial apple pie. The use of Three Dog Night, Hall and Oates, Kool and the Gang, and disco hits Americanizes Shakespeare, making his work only twenty years distant in the past rather than four hundred, and removes the language by which youth audiences are typically challenged. Dennis Kennedy observes that translations of Shakespeare into foreign languages make the texts closer to the contemporary language of London (or Los Angeles, for that matter) than to the original English.[34] "Foreign Shakespeare" tends to be much more accessible to the audience, linguistically speaking. Rock-and-roll Shakespeare treats the texts as foreign works to be translated into modern American English. Although Kennedy claims that "modernist high culture and the entrenched position of the Shakespeare industry" indicate that no translations of Shakespeare's plays into modern English will gain wide currency, production can and will do just that.[35]

One might look at these productions of rock-and-roll mediated Shakespeare in different contexts, observing different possible ways in which they reinscribe the plays, the man, and the concept of Shakespeare. First, all of the plays considered in this study fall into the category of adaptations of Shakespeare, just like Nahum Tate's *King Lear* or Tom Stoppard's *Rosencrantz and Guildenstern Are Dead*. Whereas knowledge of the original provides a different understanding of the play in the case of the latter, in the case of the former Tate does not care if his audience knows the original (and arguably would prefer that they did not). The Troubadours use music as a double referent that moves the plot, but it also substitutes for the original Shakespearean verse to make, as Tate did, a Shakespeare that is palatable to contemporary audiences. Authenticity and faithfulness to text or original conditions of production are not prioritized—playing to a popular audience on its own level through its own taste is.

Second, one might see the plays as rock musicals, particularly given the recent trend of pop musicals. In a recent article in *American Theatre* John Istel noted that for much of the twentieth century "popular music *was* theatre music"—Irving Berlin, George M. Cohan, even Rodgers and Hammerstein's music was the pop music of its day.[36] Recently, musicals have been created around the music of Abba, Billy Joel, and Randy Newman, to name but three. Baz Luhrmann's follow-up to *William Shakespeare's Romeo and Juliet* was *Moulin Rouge*, an "original" musical that used pop songs from Nirvana, T-Rex, Madonna, The Police, David Bowie, Elton John, and dozens of others. Productions such as *All's Kool That Ends Kool* simply do the same thing with Shakespeare.

Third, Troubadour Theatre Company productions represent a kind of American Shakespeare, one perhaps more original than more straightforward, "high" productions and predating the Poel-inspired Elizabethan Revival. Lawrence Levine tells of a nineteenth-century American production of Shakespeare's first comedy entitled *Ye Comedie of Errours, a Glorious Uprorious Burlesque, Not Indecorous nor Censorious, with Many a Chorus, Warrented Not to Bore Us, Now for the First Time Set Before Us.*[37] Levine argues that the idea of Shakespeare as so-called high culture is a fairly recent invention in the history of Shakespearean production, the product of Victorian attitudes toward culture. Until the twentieth century Shakespeare was popular culture and was frequently adapted into American milieus. One might consider the Troubadour productions a return to a genuinely American way of approaching Shakespeare.

Shakespeare and rock-and-roll music are now permanently mixed in American production culture, and what was so shocking to audiences in 1969 has become commonplace and even expected.[38] Rock-and-roll rebellion has become nostalgia. The music of rebellious youth is now hip-hop and rap, although these forms, too, are becoming rapidly mainstream and commercialized. In the future it is altogether possible that so-called ad-rap-tations of Shakespeare will be equally as nostalgic and commonplace. If each generation must rediscover the classics, then one of the standard methods of rediscovery and exploration of Shakespeare's plays will be to filter the texts through the popular music of those generations yet to come. I will not predict how soon we might see Britney Spears as Ophelia or hear King Lear rap out Eminem's "My Name Is . . . ," yet it will come: the readiness is all.

Notes

1. Information about *Hair* is taken from Gerome Ragni and James Rado, *Hair* (New York: Pocket Books, 1969), and from the liner notes of the rerelease of the original Broadway cast recording on compact disc (*Hair: The Original Broadway Cast Recording*, RCA Victor 1150-2-RC, 1968, 1988). See also Barbara Lee Horn, *The Age of Hair* (Westport, CT: Greenwood Press, 1991).

2. Note the similarity between "Claude" and "Claudius." Yet Claude is the Hamlet figure in this play.

3. All quotations from Shakespeare are taken from *The Riverside Shakespeare*, ed. G. Blakemore Evans (Boston: Houghton Mifflin, 1974).

4. Joseph Papp and Ted Cornell, *William Shakespeare's "Naked" Hamlet: A Production Handbook* (London: Macmillan, 1969), 40.

5. Papp and Cornell, *"Naked" Hamlet*, 41.

6. Quoted in the preface to Papp and Cornell, *"Naked" Hamlet*, 9.

7. Ibid.

8. Interestingly, a similar situation evolved out of the 1999–2000 production of *The Bomb-itty of Errors*, an "ad-rap-tation" of *The Comedy of Errors*, in which *New York Times* critic Bruce Weber slams the play as doing "damage to Shakespeare," yet he also notes that "there's a generation gap at work here. The audience seemed not to share any of my reservations and left the theatre as jazzed as any group of theatre-goers I've seen in a long time." He further observes that the house was full and that most of the audience was of college age or younger. Bruce Weber, "Rap Is to Shakespeare as Bomb Is to Comedy," *New York Times*, Dec. 21, 1999, E3.

9. John Guare, Mel Shapiro, and Galt MacDermot, *Two Gentlemen of Verona* (New York: Stein and Day, 1979).

10. Paul Friedlander, *Rock and Roll: A Social History* (Boulder, CO: Westview Press, 1996), 285.

11. Stephen M. Buhler, "Reviving Juliet, Repackaging Romeo: Transformations of Character in Pop and Post-Pop Music," in *Shakespeare after Mass Media*, ed. Richard Burt (New York: Palgrave, 2002), 243–64.

12. The rise of pop Ophelia references may be directly related to the increased connection between Ophelia and disenfranchised and alienated teenaged girls in such works as *Reviving Ophelia*, by Mary Pipher (New York: Putnam, 1994); and *Ophelia Speaks*, by Sara Shandler (New York: Harper Collins, 1999). The Ophelias and *Swamp Ophelia* predate those books, however.

13. See B. Lee Cooper and Wayne S. Haney, *Rock Music in American Popular Culture: Rock 'n' Roll Resources* (New York: Haworth, 1995) for the leveling

of references within pop lyrics. Cooper and Haney observe, "Sources such as The Holy Bible, Shakespeare's plays, and books by Lewis Carroll and Charles Dickens are freely intermingled with popular culture references" (192).

14. The irony is, of course, that the film is so much the product of Luhrmann's vision that many reviews and articles referred to it as "Baz Luhrmann's *William Shakespeare's Romeo and Juliet*."

15. Lynda E. Boose and Richard Burt, "Totally *Clueless?* Shakespeare Goes Hollywood in the 1990s," in *Shakespeare: The Movie*, ed. Lynda E. Boose and Richard Burt (London: Routledge, 1997), 17.

16. *William Shakespeare's Romeo and Juliet*, prod. Gabriella Martinelli and Baz Luhrmann, dir. Baz Luhrmann, 120 min., Twentieth Century Fox, 1997, videocassette.

17. *William Shakespeare's Romeo and Juliet: Music from the Motion Picture*, Capitol Records CDP8 37715 0, 1996; and *William Shakespeare's Romeo and Juliet: Music from the Motion Picture: Volume 2*, Capitol Records CDP72438 55567 2 2, 1997.

18. Donald Lyons, "Lights, Camera, Shakespeare," *Commentary* 103, no. 2 (Feb. 1997): 57–60.

19. James N. Loehlin, "'These Violent Delights Have Violent Ends': Baz Luhrmann's Millennial Shakespeare," in *Shakespeare, Film, Fin de Siècle*, ed. Mark Thornton Burnett and Ramona Wray (New York: St. Martin's, 2000), 123–24.

20. We might also note, however, that the vast majority of music used in the film is not rock but opera, classical music (Wagner, Faure, Mozart, etc.), Gregorian chant, and other forms of music. The film sites itself in the rock world, but the focus by critics and MTV—not to mention that the rock music is on the sound tracks, whereas the classical music is not—makes Luhrmann's film seem much more rock-oriented than it actually is. Mozart and Wagner have as much to do with shaping the soundscape of the film as One Inch Punch and the Butthole Surfers.

21. Mary Lindroth, "The Prince and the Newscaster: Baz Luhrmann Updates Shakespeare for a Y2K Audience," http://www.middleenglish.org/spc/spcissues/22.3/lindroth.html (accessed Dec. 1, 2003).

22. Loehlin, "Violent Delights," 123.

23. Luhrmann's film attempts to site Shakespeare not in high culture but in popular culture. Yet even it is seen as high popular culture. Troma Entertainment, a low-budget studio known for such films as *The Toxic Avenger, Class of Nuke 'em High*, and *Sgt Kabukiman, N.Y.P.D.*, produced *Tromeo and Juliet* (prod. Lloyd Kaufman and Michael Herz, dir. Lloyd Kaufman, 100 min., Troma Entertainment, 1997, videocassette), featuring "all the body-piercing, dismemberment, and car chases Shakespeare always wanted, but never had" (Luhrmann interview on the videotape). Like Luhrmann's film, the sound track is filled with songs from rock groups such as Sublime, Motorhead, the Ass Ponys, and Unsane. Whereas Luhrmann's film is musically located in alternative pop and dance music, Troma's film is clearly in the world of punk and heavy metal. Kaufman underscores this fact by using Lemmy Killmeister, lead guitarist and

singer of Motorhead, as the chorus. Like in Luhrmann's film, written text identifies the members of the cast as they are shown. As the chorus, speaking obviously in Times Square, intones his speech, the onscreen text states "Lemmy: House of Motorhead," equating the band with the Capulets and Montagues. Much of the Troma film parodies the Luhrmann film. Whereas Baz seeks seriousness in his employment of popular culture, Troma revels in B-movie excesses of sex and violence and shows far more edge than *William Shakespeare's Romeo and Juliet*, even though it is equally distant from mainstream culture.

24. Quoted in Jon Lewis, *The Road to Romance and Ruin: Teen Films and Youth Culture* (New York: Routledge, 1992), 100. In the case of the commercialization of rock and pop music we might note that all eighteen tracks of Moby's technopop album *Play* were licensed for commercial usage before the album was even released. The acquisition of the Beatles catalog by Michael Jackson was followed by the licensing of "Revolution" for use by Nike shoes in its commercials. Both classical rock and new rock music are rapidly being used to endorse products and services.

25. I am indebted to one of the *Theatre Symposium* editorial board members who juried this paper for pointing out this context.

26. Bob Carlton, *Return to the Forbidden Planet* (London: Methuen, 1985).

27. Much information on the group can be found on their Web site, http://www.troubie.com, including the group's mission statement, a history, and several reviews (accessed Feb. 15, 2003).

28. It should be noted that even in the Troubies' non-Shakespearean productions, the bard is never far from the troupe's stage or rock culture. In *Funky Punks with Junk in Their Trunks*, a circus-based piece that features clowning, acrobatics, and sketch comedy, one sketch, entitled "The Funky Punks Watch TV," has channel surfing clowns switch back and forth between "Masterpiece Theatre's *Romeo and Juliet*" and MTV's *TRL* (although both are performed by the same set of clowns) until the two begin to blend.

29. Joel Beers, "And Now for Something Completely Different," *Orange County Weekly*, July 16, 1999, 29.

30. Some material about the production comes from reviews. See Richard Schulenberg, "Troubadour's 'Twelfth Dog Night' at Miles Is 'The Funniest Show in Town,'" *Santa Monica Mirror*, Aug. 18–24, 1999, n.p.; Terri Roberts, "Twelfth Dog Night," *Daily Variety*, Dec. 21, 1999, 14; and Beers, "Completely Different," 29.

31. See Julio Martinez, "All's Kool That Ends Kool," *Daily Variety*, May 23, 2002, 12.

32. Quoted in Clara Sturak, "Shakespeare's Stayin' Alive with New Production at Miles Playhouse," *Santa Monica Mirror*, July 19–25, 2000, 12.

33. Boose and Burt, "Totally *Clueless*?" 13.

34. Dennis Kennedy, "Shakespeare without His Language," *Shakespeare, Theory, and Performance*, ed. James C. Bulman (London: Routledge, 1996), 136–37.

35. In fact, one can argue that all productions, even those that use the original texts unedited, "translate" the original language by adding other semiotics

(set, costume, video, music, gesture, tone, etc.) to signify in a manner that alters the meaning of the original text. One might not understand the exact meaning of a particular phrase, but in production the meaning (original or new) is made clear as a result of additional signs.

36. John Istel, "Pop Goes the Musical," *American Theatre*, 20, no. 3 (Mar. 2003): 21–25.

37. Lawrence Levine, *Highbrow/Lowbrow: The Emergence of Cultural Hierarchy in America* (Cambridge, MA: Harvard University Press, 1988), 14.

38. The author himself, it should be noted, is guilty of employing rock music in academic and professional productions of Shakespeare's plays, from *Richard III* to *The Tempest* to other Elizabethan and Jacobean productions. And he'll do it again, too.

The Falstaff Project

Redescribing a World

Sarah Ferguson and Annie Smith

[Shakespeare's] works are no longer being presented to a Canadian audience from a British aesthetic. They are now being directed by theatre artists who have grown up theatrically with the Canadian voice at the forefront of our consciousness or have developed in a theatrical environment that has always had access to the Canadian voice. The approach to and perspective of these productions is Canadian.

—Stephen Heatley, "Adapting Shakespeare to the Prairie Landscape"

T HE *FALSTAFF PROJECT*, a Canadian rewriting of William Shakespeare's *Henry IV*, parts 1 and 2, was produced at the University of British Columbia, Frederic Wood Theatre, November 14–23, 2002. The prologue written for this production prepares the audience, in a humorous way, for the considerable liberties the writer has taken with the work of the Bard. The prologue also addresses issues of authenticity, adaptation, and ethics that were raised during the 2003 SETC Symposium, "Elizabethan Performance in North American Spaces." In this introduction Philostrate is the Master of Revels dressed as Elton John, and Shakespeare is played by the writer, Errol Durbach, dressed in Elizabethan costume:

PHILOSTRATE: Ah, Master Shakespeare! Welcome to the court.
Her Majesty, of late, has been distraught
By the dumbing down and dullness of our stage.
"Summon up the Bard," quoth she. "Engage
Him for a season! Commission something grand.
Let's advertise a play 'By Royal Command.'"
SHAKESPEARE: My Lord of Revels, must we needs converse
In tedious ta-dums of rhyming verse?
I'm sick of it. I flatly must reject it.

PHILOSTRATE: The Queen, however, surely will expect it:
The light and lively diastolic beat
Of rhyme that glides on pentametric feet . . .
SHAKESPEARE: Ridiculous! Grotesque! Do you suppose
That Falstaff speaks in aught but prose?
PHILOSTRATE: "Falstaff" did I hear you say?
Are you thinking of another Falstaff play?
I abominate your *Merry Wives of Windsor*!
For though your Knight be fat—your plot is thin, sir.
SHAKESPEARE: I have in mind a *Henry IV* rerun.
The Histories played in sequence? Could be fun . . .
PHILOSTRATE: Hmmm . . . Too long. Winkle out the Falstaff bits
And concentrate upon the tavern skits.
SHAKESPEARE: Chop my texts? Cut scenes? Condense? Rewrite??
PHILOSTRATE: Why not?—Send for Durbach! Send for Wright!
They'll edit Henry Four Parts One and Two.
If Ibsen could endure it, so can you![1]

So, what is the "Canadian voice"? For this production it is a critical
voice, a self-conscious voice of a national entity whose world position
is to be caught always between larger political powers. As Canadians
fondly believe, our critical vision is clearer as we detach from the powers
that squeeze us culturally through our own unique history; our huge,
sparsely inhabited spaces; and our own polite ironical nature. As Linda
Burnett explains in her article "Redescribing a World":

> Canadian playwrights certainly do use Shakespeare's plays for applied poli-
> tics. . . . But what is really significant about these playwrights' endeavor is
> their refusal to start a new picture from scratch. Instead of painting over
> Shakespeare's work, they touch it up some places and in others add their
> own representations to stand beside his. In so doing, they are engaged
> in the constructive postcolonial project that [Salman] Rushdie calls "re-
> describing a world."[2]

Errol Durbach's approach to writing his adaptation exemplifies Burnett's thoughts. Rather than starting from scratch, Durbach continues Shakespeare's process of condensing historical events. Shakespeare
worked to "chronicle the government of England from Richard II to
Henry V—a formidable terrain covering the assassination of Richard,
civil warfare, the uneasy reign of Henry IV, and the career of the Prince
of Wales who will become a national hero and lead his army against the
French."[3] Durbach winnows the Bard's tetralogy of History Plays even
further, resulting in a 2.5-hour-long play that intersperses sections of
the original texts among newly written verse. The prologue excerpt

provided here illustrates Durbach's intention to "rerun" *Henry IV* in contemporary fashion, with "chops," "cuts," "condensations," and "rewrites." With the deliberate employment of contemporary theatrical devices such as media coverage and pointed anachronism, *The Falstaff Project* does indeed "redescribe a world."

In an interview conducted for an undergraduate class, Durbach reveals his intentions when asked by interviewer Marek Czuma, "Why do this project?"

> The point about the Henry plays is that the first one is very, very well written. The second one is not. Therefore, when you go to the theatre you tend to see Part I of *Henry IV* and very seldom see Part II which means that you see half a career which is half the career of Falstaff and half the career of Hal and half of their relationship. And so what you see, in fact, is a truncated play. You don't see the complete, dynamic movement of a relationship, or a character, or a career.[4]

The resulting play illustrates how a Canadian writer uses both original and Shakespearean text to redescribe the complete world of Hal and Falstaff and how this act of redescribing can inform the production's set, costume, and video designs. This essay discusses these production elements and the script using the lens of Burnett's "constructive postcolonial project."

Much of Durbach's impetus for *The Falstaff Project* was the actual world situation at the time of writing and producing the play. To his mind the grooming of a son to become a Machiavellian ruler mirrors the contemporary dynastic situation in many countries of the world—East and West. He sees one of the themes of the work as "clearly political." The "discourses on power, authority, rule" are there in the original text.[5]

In the months since the play was produced, world events have continued to play out many of the dynamics explored within *The Falstaff Project*. This contemporary reality of politics, conflict, and the desire for power is not so different from the reality facing England in the 1400s, the time of the Henrys; the 1700s, the reign of Elizabeth I; or Tony Blair's government today.

Robert Gardiner's set design offered the spatial opportunity "to create new texts in which the old stories are re-imagined and reinterpreted."[6] The stage was divided into two parts separated by a scrim at the proscenium that ran the full width of the stage. This division became the physical manifestation of the parallel worlds and the parallel narratives of two fathers, Henry IV and Falstaff. The proscenium stage worked well for the design concept by providing a physical frame for the upstage that suggested the framing of a television set. This framing subtly suggested the interconnectedness of power and media today and let this image stand beside Shakespeare's representations of power and control.

The upper stage, behind the scrim, was predominantly the world of politics and government, although it was also used as a "neutral space," becoming at times Gad's Hill Common and the Shrewsbury battlefield. The scrim was sometimes an invisible fourth wall that allowed a clear view of the government workings, sometimes a semitransparent screen on which images were projected and the news clips were shown that masked or framed the world of politics, and sometimes a black void that was used as a backdrop for the forestage scenes. Always hovering over the entire stage was a row of golden skulls. These skulls would sometimes catch the light as they haunted the action of the play. Although Wright would not directly comment on his interpretation of these skulls, the audience remarked on them in a variety of ways, calling them "ghosts in the closet," "masks," and "trophies."

The space in front of the scrim extended forward from the proscenium to the edge of the stage, and then another lower level was built in front of that. This area was the world of Mistress Quickly's tavern and, at one point in the play, Shallow's orchard. One could enter the tavern from small ramps on either side connected to the stage proper or through a trap door in the floor. The tavern was below the level of the stage so that the stage made a partial wall that was used as part of the set. The furnishings were rough and suggested that the tavern was set in Renaissance times, although the costumes of the "low-life" characters were more contemporary. In this staging Shakespeare's Renaissance world was clearly positioned beside (or in this case in front of) a Canadian contemporary world in order to reimagine and reinterpret the perspective offered.[7]

The action shifted rapidly between the two worlds: Westminster and the tavern. Prince Hal was always aware of the two worlds. Even when he was physically in the tavern, he could participate in a scene happening in the palace. This visual and physical splitting and reuniting of worlds is the metatheatrical structure on which the play is built and experiments with postcolonial ideas regarding disassembling and reassembling to "advance narratives to stand beside . . . earlier narratives . . . to *counter-balance* those earlier univocal narratives."[8] A stage direction reads: "'Split-screen' effect: both Falstaff and the King occupy parallel positions in their respective worlds, and the Prince faces forwards—he could be in the 'real' presence of either man, until he assumes his father's role in the tavern play."[9]

Director John Wright, when explaining his thoughts about Hal, provides the relationship between his ideas and the visual image created by Gardiner: "I tend to see him [Hal] as being able to hold two positions in his mind at one time and do justice to them both. One is the Machiavellian notion that he will manipulate, but the other is the notion of his pleasure actually in the company of Falstaff and his sense of loss ultimately when he thinks Falstaff has died."[10]

Costume designer Marti Wright's work is also an example of Burnett's theory about Canada's relationship to Shakespeare and the postcolonial project. Wright refused to start from scratch and tackled the plays' themes by creating costumes that were a mélange of periods, styles, and classes. Wright discusses her process in *A Companion Guide to The Falstaff Project*: "In an effort to encompass all wars, initial thoughts ranged from retro to futuristic, from *Chimes at Midnight* to *Road Warrior*. . . . We found ourselves lurking between 1910 and 1980. . . . Wishing to avoid specific armies, ranks, countries, etc., in any one uniform, we chose them all and mixed them up."[11]

The weapons used continued this motif. Swords, knives, rifles, and pistols were employed simultaneously. The common soldiers carried firearms of different vintages, and on occasion an Uzi-type of automatic weapon was also evident. The nobility, on the other hand, fought with broadswords because director John Wright felt they were "a symbol of honour."[12] In this production, however, Hotspur is killed in the middle of a broadsword charge when Hal casually raises a pistol and fires. This makes material the death of honor, as symbolized through the sword, by the agency of the common man's pistol in the hands of the future king. The callousness of Hal's act bespeaks assassination rather than chivalrous combat.

The costumes of the tavern characters, which were also a mix of styles and periods, were contemporary and casual in feeling. This combination juxtaposed nicely with the sense of the Renaissance period created by the rustic tavern setting. The sense of present-day informality also made these characters more accessible to the audience as a whole, which was composed in large part of university students. Interestingly, this accessibility could possibly mirror a connection made by the tavern characters and the groundling component of the audience in Shakespeare's time.

The characters of the court also wore contemporary dress but in the more formal style of dress pants and suits. The formality set their class apart from the more casual "low-life" tavern characters. The court world made use of contemporary artifacts, such as cell phones and television, and was also captured in the realistic news videos that were used extensively throughout the play.

The video design by Amos Hertzman brought in contemporary images to stand beside Shakespeare's historical ones. Here technology became a creative element in its own right. There was extensive use of projections, on the scrim that horizontally divided the stage's two playing areas, to frame the events in the world of royalty. A slide of Westminster was shown during the teleconference between Northumberland and Henry IV with each man seen through the scrim standing in his own square of light. An image of Glendower Castle was similarly used during the scene depicting Hotspur, Glendower, Mortimer, and Douglas in Wales. A particularly effective use of a projection had an excerpt from the text of Machiavelli's *The Prince* on the scrim while Henry IV was plainly seen plotting behind it. Specially created slides were also projected to provide context and setting, such as a forest path down which the soldiers marched and an orchard in bloom.

Hertzman's design also connected the past century of war to the world of the play. Archival photographs of soldiers from World War I to Vietnam were projected in a slow dissolve sequence onto the scrim while the Battle of Shrewsbury was clearly fought behind it. This overlapping of eras created a wonderful sense of timelessness both within the play and within the idea of war itself. At one point the scrim was raised, and the projection fell onto the stage floor, across the actors themselves, and continued up the cyclorama at the back of the stage. The effect was breathtaking as the photographs of past soldiers were projected onto the present soldiers of the play, who in turn represent soldiers from a more distant past.

Durbach and Hertzman created a new metaperspective on the action of the play that further situates this production as a "constructive postcolonial project." They created a televised news service: Network News. This creation took the events of the play and presented them within the contemporary news-show format. Each takeoff began with opening graphics and theme music and then showed announcers trading off stories in contemporary fashion both within the "studio" and with reporters "in the field." These newscasts are interspersed throughout the play, bringing the events from Scotland, Wales, and the battlefield onto the scrim, and into our living rooms, as it were.

The obvious construction of the Network News was a brilliant strategy to provoke us, as audience, to reflect on what we were seeing in front of us onstage, both the construction of the play itself and the construction of history the play presented. It also allowed us to reflect on what we see happening on our TV screens in our own homes. Comments from seminar students proved the effectiveness of this element of the production as they made cross-references from the political dynamics of the English court of Henry IV and V to the current political dynamics before the declaration of war on Iraq. The projected images on the scrim served as a literal "smoke screen" behind which the real machinations of the state occurred.

Burnett's concept of parallel narratives was strongly emphasized when the news reporters spoke a mix of original Shakespearean verse and created text. The overt heightened language of the iambic pentameter parodied the contemporary heightened language of newspeak with its deliberate use of inflammatory terms and rhetoric such as "weapons of mass destruction," "axis of evil," and "coalition of the willing."

The following text from Durbach's adaptation gives a clear example of the parallel narratives. The newscast is based on Sir Richard Vernon's report to the rebel leaders in 1 *Henry IV,* act 4, scene 1. The underlined segments are taken verbatim from Shakespeare's text but reorganized somewhat. The phrase "King in person" has been changed to "Prince in person" to focus directly on the dialectic of honor and expedience embodied by Hotspur and Hal. The reporter plays the role of Vernon in reverse, seeking information rather than giving it:

TV ANNOUNCER: This report just in from our War Correspondent in the North.

[The following video clip takes place in front of a tank and a few soldiers. The sounds of helicopters passing overhead are heard occasionally. The video shows the War Correspondent with microphone and Hotspur in battle gear.]

WC: The news from Wales is that Glendower's troops
Have been delayed for up to fourteen days.

(Hotspur emerges from the tent.)

Here's Hotspur, leader of the rebel troops—
This information <u>bears a frosty sound.</u>
<u>Is't not the worst tidings heard of yet?</u>

HOT: <u>What may the King's whole battle reach unto?</u>
<u>Thirty thousand? Forty let it be!!</u>
<u>My father and Glendower being both away,</u>
<u>The powers of us may serve so great a day!</u>

WC: And further we have learned the <u>Prince in person</u>
Is hitherwards intended speedily
<u>With strong and mighty preparation.</u>

HOT: <u>The madcap Prince of Wales? He shall be welcome, too,</u>
And all his comrades from the city stews.
<u>Let them come like sacrifices in their trim—</u>
<u>All hot and bleeding will we offer them</u>
To the God of smoke and war! <u>I am on fire</u>
<u>To hear this rich reprisal is so nigh.</u>

WC: What impels you, Sir, to wage this war?

HOT: Honour!—well-respected honour bids me on.
Honour drives me like a thunderbolt
<u>Against the bosom of this Prince of Wales—</u>
Yea, though we swim <u>up to the ears in blood!</u>

WC: Thank you, Sir! Back to Gerald Vanderwoude. . . .

TV ANNOUNCER: Stay tun'd to this channel for news reports on the progress of the conflict at Shrewsbury.[13]

The TV then fades out, as Hotspur and Douglas take the stage for a
quick review of their strategy.

Durbach developed two significant dialectics, two parallel narratives,
in his adaptation. The first dialectic is one of honor and expedience
personified by the two sons, Hotspur and Hal. The second dialectic is
one of order and misrule embodied by the two "fathers," Henry IV
and Falstaff. The physical design of the production, of two worlds, em-
beds the dialectics in the action of the play. Durbach sees the meaning
of the play in its structure. Prince Hal makes a calculated choice to
reject the "Falstaff principle" of anarchy and embraces the order and
deception of Henry IV. There is no synthesis. Durbach's vision of King
Henry V is not the vision of Kenneth Branagh or Sir Lawrence Olivier.
This new king is Machiavellian to the core. With his rejection of Falstaff
the vitality of pleasure, camaraderie, gross villainy, and excess is ex-
changed for media image, sophisticated deceit, terror, and wrath. Durbach writes about "the archetypal relationship of fathers and sons: the
Prince's fractured allegiance to (at least) two models of fatherhood, two
ways of engaging with the world, two demands upon his self-definition"
and fears that "what we must deny in the process of political maturity—

the Falstaff principle—often leaves us humanly diminished and, in Prince Henry's case, even more terrifying than Henry IV as Political Man."[14]

As powerful as this production was, there was one noticeable difference between it and other Canadian adaptations of Shakespeare's works. As in the original texts, the female characters are tantalizingly underplayed. Whereas many Canadian adaptations have chosen to develop the female parallel narratives beyond what Shakespeare gives us (notably Ann Marie McDonald's *Goodnight Desdemona; Good Morning Juliet*, Margaret Clarke's *Gertrude & Ophelia*, and Normand Chaurette's *The Queens*),[15] Durbach has kept the women characters more ornamental than agential. His project has offered a new perspective of a political world that continues to be dominated by patriarchal values.

The Falstaff Project, as a postcolonial project, critiques Shakespeare's original text and our contemporary acceptance of the Machiavellian ethos in world affairs. The counternarrative of Falstaff's principle of self-gratification balances the master narrative of "might makes right." Curiously, both poles of the dialectic shadow each other because both are based on the supremacy of the individual. Durbach's intention to clarify political and moral ambivalence also corresponds to the goals Burnett sees in constructive postcolonialism:

> [T]hese Canadian adaptations of Shakespeare offer social and political commentary. . . . But these adaptations do something more, something best understood in terms of the differences between a deconstructive postmodernism and constructive postcolonialism, the most significant of which is that postcolonialism—because of the way it views the subject and history—has a "distinct political agenda," . . . while postmodernism is "politically ambivalent." Whereas postmodernism uses irony simply to tear down, postcolonialism uses it both to disassemble and to reassemble.[16]

There are ironies inherent to the original plays, ironies in adapting them to relate to this current historical time. These ironies are played on throughout Durbach's adaptation—for example, in the juxtaposition of created and original text and in the design choices for set, costumes, and props. The most overt deployment of irony is in the use of media—the icons, the jingles, the invasion of private space, and the staging of news. This disassembling and reassembling of characters, settings, and language goes beyond deconstruction to create a powerful Canadian narrative to counterbalance the master narrative assumed to be the "authentic" Shakespeare.

Notes

1. Errol Durbach, *The Falstaff Project*, University of British Columbia, Department of Theatre, http://www.theatre.ubc.ca/images/falstaff_script.pdf (accessed Sep. 3, 2003). The mention of Ibsen in the final line alludes to a previous collaboration between Durbach and director John Wright on an adaptation of *Peer Gynt*.

2. Linda Burnett, "Redescribing a World: Towards a Theory of Shakespearean Adaptation in Canada," *Canadian Theatre Review* 111 (2002): 9.

3. Errol Durbach, *A Companion Guide to* The Falstaff Project, http://www.theatre.ubc.ca/images/studyguide_falstaff_project_72.pdf (accessed Sep. 3, 2003), 4.

4. Errol Durbach and John Wright, interview by Marek Czuma, Sarah Ferguson, and Annie Smith, DVD recording, November 2002, Department of Theatre, University of British Columbia.

5. Durbach, *Companion Guide,* 4.

6. Burnett, "Redescribing a World," 6.

7. Ibid.

8. Ibid., 7.

9. Durbach, *Falstaff Project*, 20.

10. Wright, interview.

11. Marti Wright, "The Falstaff Project," in *A Companion Guide to The Falstaff Project*, ed. Errol Durbach, Alison Green, John Wright, and Linda Fenton Malloy (Vancouver: Theatre at UBC, 2002), 7; also available online at http://www.theatre.ubc.ca/images/studyguide_falstaff_project_72.pdf (accessed Sep. 3, 2003), 7.

12. Ibid.

13. Durbach, *Falstaff Project*, 35–36.

14. Durbach, *Companion Guide,* 4.

15. See Daniel Fischlin, "Theatrical Adaptations of Shakespeare in Canada: A Working Bibliography," *Canadian Theatre Review* 111 (2002): 69–73.

16. Burnett, "Redescribing a World," 6.

The De-evolution of a Tradition

The Elizabethan Theatre at
the Oregon Shakespeare Festival

Susan S. Cole and Richard L. Hay

THE IDEA OF Shakespearean plays staged in reproductions of the Elizabethan public playhouse was a concept that became fully realized during the twentieth century. By the late nineteenth century there had been some experiments in first simplifying the staging of Shakespeare and finally in utilizing scenic reproductions of the Elizabethan public playhouse set within the traditional picture-frame stage. By early in the twentieth century reproductions were being built outdoors, and Shakespearean plays were performed in facilities somewhat like the original theatres. In the middle to late twentieth century the reproductions were built as a part of freestanding enclosed replicas of the Elizabethan public playhouse, and scholars, students, and the public became fascinated by the idea of seeing the plays as originally staged. The original intent of the attempts to produce Shakespeare on a replica stage was to enhance the audience's understanding of the plays and to restore the scripts to their original form, eliminating the "improvements" of the seventeenth, eighteenth, and nineteenth centuries.

"Modified Elizabethan staging" was a phrase used by English director B. Iden Payne, a disciple of William Poel's nineteenth-century Shakespearean productions, and referred to a practice used in several theatres where he directed during the early twentieth century. Payne was at the University of Washington in the summer of 1930, where he directed a production of *Love's Labor's Lost* using "modified Elizabethan staging" designed by his former student John Conway. He also directed during the first four seasons at a summer Shakespeare Festival in San Diego from 1949 to 1952 and directed at the Oregon Shakespearean Festival during the 1956 and 1961 seasons.

A young teacher, Angus Bowmer, had acted in the Payne production of *Love's Labor's Lost* at Washington "during which I fell in love with Mr. Payne's 'modified Elizabethan staging' of Shakespeare."[1] Bowmer went on to teach at the Southern Oregon Normal School in tiny Ashland, Oregon, where he created a "modified Elizabethan" stage set on the proscenium stage for a production of *The Merchant of Venice* in 1934. Encouraged by the success of the production, Bowmer, along with some friends and collaborators, planned a Shakespearean festival to be presented as a part of the Fourth of July celebration held within the walls of the old Chautauqua circle in Ashland. The production of *Merchant* was revived for two performances along with a single performance of *Twelfth Night*. The program optimistically stated that this was "The First Annual Shakespearean Festival."[2] The plays were so successful that Angus Bowmer continued to produce Shakespeare during the following summers. The season consisted of three plays for two years and in 1937 officially became the Oregon Shakespearean Festival.[3]

Bowmer's list of the things the festival would be and not be "might well be called the 'Oregon Shakespearean Festival Manifesto'" and established what became the Ashland style of producing Shakespeare. Among the items on the list: "It should be a people's theatre, that is it should belong to the audience," and "it should be unique without being quixotic. . . . It should not be a theatre in which the talents of any one theatrical artist are exploited to the detriment of either the audience's enjoyment or the playwright's intent; it should not have the clinical aura of academia; it should not be a museum."[4]

Bowmer's intention was to produce Shakespearean plays much as they must have been produced in the sixteenth and seventeenth centuries but within the conventions of Payne's modified Elizabethan staging. Bowmer pointed out that some directors feel that it is impossible to recreate a sixteenth- or seventeenth-century audience and that the plays must be reinterpreted to reflect the current society and world. According to Frank Hildy, referring to the London Globe Theatre, they are "translating it [the play] for modern audiences not expanding the world of the audience."[5]

"When the producers of such productions find credible 17th Century parallels in modern life, they can beget viable productions," said Bowmer. "When they skew Shakespeare's intent . . . or when they produce only for novelty or shock, they do a disservice to their audiences and to their producing companies. On Ashland's Elizabethan stage, however, such productions should be inconceivable. The same sort of research that led to the construction of that stage should become a renewed search for the ways in which Shakespeare and his contemporaries used it."[6] It should be noted that in contrast to today's archaeological and theoretical research into the form and look of the Elizabethan stage, Bowmer built his theatre and principles of production on second- and third-hand ideas.

The first stage for the Oregon Shakespearean Festival was built in 1935 within the abandoned roofless walls of the Chautauqua dome that caught Bowmer's attention because of their resemblance to the Globe Theatre in old drawings. The city agreed to build a permanent architectural facade based on the elements that Bowmer remembered from the stage setting at the University of Washington. It was initially an unpainted wood-planked architectural facade with a main stage between two penthouse columns with a curtain between. There were also two side stages, each with entrance doorways and window balconies over, as well as an "inner below" and an "inner above." There was no third-level gallery. The penthouse roof extended from stage right to stage left, supported centrally by the columns, creating the effect of a proscenium stage with a forestage extending under the sky, the full width of which equaled the main-stage width but with slightly tapering sides. In addition, the two inner stages had front curtains creating two small proscenium stages in the facade. The so-called main-stage or penthouse curtains were operated in full view of the audience by costumed "curtain pages." The central penthouse curtains allowed properties to be preset while scenes were being played on the forestage. The "pages," who were often young women, either remained behind the columns or sat on the sides of the stage. The side stages were sometimes also used as small pictorial proscenium stages. For instance, a sky drop framed by a cutout foliage border and wings silhouetted forest scenes in the 1939 production of *As You Like It*.[7] In 1940 the original stage was partially burned along with the six years' accumulation of costumes. Despite the damage, the season went on with actors in street clothes playing to eighteen hundred people. The building was razed, and the festival was dark for five years during World War II.[8]

A new theatre was opened in 1947, built from plans that Bowmer drew from tracings he had made of John Conway's proposed Elizabethan stage for the University of Washington based on the dimensions of the Peter Street contract for the Fortune Theatre. The rectangular shape of the stage implied in the Fortune contract was not adopted in favor of a forty-five-degree tapered forestage that recalled the John

Cranford Adams reconstruction of the Globe published in 1942. The forestage extended forward from the fifty-five-foot-wide principal stage area. The front of the forestage projected 27½ feet beyond the facade. The principal playing areas also included the main- or middle-stage area between the two penthouse columns; two lateral side stages, each between a penthouse column; and the side wall of the facade, set at forty-five degrees and incorporating doorways with casement windows above, again recalling Adams.

The audience faced the stage in nearly straight rows of seating barely wider than the penthouse columns, giving the audience a direct, frontal view of the performance. The resulting sight lines allowed the penthouse curtains to mask extensive property and scenic changes during forestage scenes. Often complete interior or exterior settings, with sky drops, were revealed in the inner stage. Sometimes, stairs were set up to connect the inner above to the main stage, or extensive platforming was set up on the middle or main-stage area. Other changeable decorations were confined to the areas that could be concealed by the penthouse or inner-stage curtains.[9]

Growth in the popularity of the festival in the 1950s required an expansion of the seating area. First the seating was widened with the straight row side sections paralleling the forty-five-degree angle of the forestage. Sight lines from the end seats were extended far outside the penthouse columns, putting property setups behind the penthouse curtains in view of some audience members. The penthouse columns blocked the good sight lines into the inner stages for the side seats. For the distant audience members the inner stages had become too remote to be used as acting areas, and there was a change in attitude regarding the appropriateness of using these spaces as scenic stages.

The conventions of the picture-frame stage, including the penthouse curtains, were gradually eliminated, with the rejection of the use of painted box sets and sky drops in the "inner below" as being inappropriate to the Elizabethan style of staging. However, the inner below was used for the setting of props and furniture, such as thrones against neutral curtains, for years later. The eventual elimination of the penthouse or main-stage curtains between the penthouse columns opened up the whole stage to view and ended the nineteenth-century picture-frame tradition. The curtains, however, occasionally persisted briefly into the 1960s in the third version of the Elizabethan stage. They last appeared in 1961 for the production of *All's Well That Ends Well*, complete with curtain pages.

Success and the need for more seating facilitated an increase to twelve hundred seats, many too far from the stage, far beyond the limits of

The third Oregon Shakespearean Festival Elizabethan playhouse, opened in 1959. The playhouse is still in use with the addition of an audience enclosure and balcony and changes to the seating. Photo by the authors.

the Fortune Theatre, and hence reduced the effectiveness of the inner stages and the balcony of the "inner above." In an effort to bring the area used to "reveal" scenes further downstage, since the inner below was too remote if the penthouse curtains were not used, a structure was placed in front of the inner below on the main stage. This structure, inspired by C. Walter Hodges's sketch for the monument scene in *Antony and Cleopatra*, provided an acting area in front of the inner above, but eighteen inches lower, and a "reveal" space below that, which could be concealed by a *u*-shaped curtain.[10] This structure, called the pavilion, was created in response to the problem of revealing Desdemona's bed in a midstage position without the penthouse curtains to conceal the setup. Initially, the pavilion was not used in every production in a season and was removed for the "traditional" staging of the other plays. This pavilion brought the "above" scenes closer to audience and actors on the main-stage level.

The longer season and more exacting technical requirements necessitated additions to the theatre, including additional backstage areas. In the early 1950s the basement was excavated,

exposing inadequate foundations of the original concrete walls, and neces-
sitating replacement of the old supporting posts and removal of an already
cracked foundation under the penthouse pillars. . . . The accumulation of
remodeling and years has resulted in a seriously weakened building, with
the back part lower than the front and a somewhat swaybacked "inner
above." Much of this was occasioned by the constantly increasing need for
space, but some of it, particularly the complete excavation of the basement,
was necessitated by the condemnation by the State Fire Marshall of all
upstairs dressing rooms and much of the wiring.[11]

In 1958 the haphazard building was condemned, and in 1959 it was
replaced. Richard L. Hay designed the new Elizabethan theatre and
based the building on the previous stage and its traditions of use and
the John Cranford Adams reconstruction. No traditional seventeenth-
century building methods or materials were used. The half-timbering
was achieved by the superficial application of one-inch boards. The facade and audience were still contained within the Chautauqua circle. A
third gallery, the "musicians' gallery," was added to the new theatre,
along with space for scenic and costume construction. The slope in the
audience seating area was increased to improve sight lines. Later in the
late 1960s a major seating remodel created an arced amphitheatre with
gently stepped terraces.

A removable pavilion was a part of this new structure and could be
changed nightly for each production. There was a "short pavilion" and
the "long pavilion" with more space within the curtained area, as well
as above it. Changeable pavilion curtains became important scenic elements. The pavilion pushed inner scenes closer to the audience and allowed for the introduction of other scenic and mechanical elements.
Whole scenes were rarely played within the pavilion except for bed
scenes and the start of some table scenes or a throne. In the 1963 production of *Romeo and Juliet* a slip stage was introduced into the raised
pavilion floor that made it possible to set up the tomb behind the curtains and then thrust the unit forward onto the main stage. Other productions used the slip stage for thrones and other units. Scenic elements
and properties became more elaborate within the reveal space of the
pavilion or when thrust forward even more on the slip stage, which
allowed for the use of such units in the midstage area of the main stage
yet allowed them to be set up out of sight of the audience.

The 1959 playhouse still stands but has undergone a number of
changes and adjustments demanded by modern staging attitudes. The
pavilion is no longer changed, but other structural elements are used.
Stairways are built for some productions to connect to the "above"

spaces. There may be either a single or double stair to either side of the inner above. In the 1959 stage facade actors exited the "above" spaces and traveled to the first level by interior stairs behind the facade. With the addition of onstage stairs, actors make the transition in sight of the audience and become a part of the stage picture at various levels on the stairs. The use of the inner above has been minimized except as it exists as the upper part of the staircase.

Since Bowmer's retirement, in 1971, there has been a change in the approach to the use of the Shakespearean stage. Originally, a group of directors and designers who worked with the festival over a number of years adhered to the Bowmer style of production. When the festival had a single performance space, the Elizabethan theatre, single costume and scenic designers were each responsible for the entire season. One of these long-term festival members is principal scenic and theatre designer Richard L. Hay, who started as a student on the lighting crew in 1950 and was hired in 1953 as scenic designer and technical director. Since that time he has designed the entire Shakespearean canon and all four of the present theatres.

Shakespearean plays are also performed in the two indoor theatres, and the style of Shakespearean production in these theatres is often more modern or postmodern. The Bowmer Theatre opened in 1970 and has an open stage, and The Black Swan opened in 1977 with a three-quarter-thrust arrangement. The Black Swan was replaced in 2002 with the flexible New Theatre that can be configured into arena, thrust, or alley settings. Said Richard Hay in 1995:

> I think the way a lot of theatres go down is because the theatre is less important to the artistic director than the artistic director's own ego—so some artistic directors hazard their own theatres in the expression of their own wishes . . . but in our case, most of the people who work for this theatre are not using it as a vehicle for their own ego or for their own advancement or as a stepping stone to something else. They contribute to this theatre to sustain it rather than to use it. I think that's one of the important reasons it has continued.[12]

The seating area was renovated in 1992 and a covered balcony, the Allen Pavilion, was added to improve lighting positions and block environmental noise. The city of Ashland had grown, and the traffic and the sounds of people and ducks in nearby Lithia Park often intruded on the performances. The addition of the balcony still within the Chautauqua walls gave a different perspective for those seated there and made the three-dimensional quality of the stage more apparent. Unfortunately, the angled, raised sight line also lengthened the view from the rear of the balcony. The slope of the orchestra seats was increased and the audience effectively wrapped further around the forestage. The changed seating areas also impacted on the stage itself. The greatest change was the addition of vomitoria to allow actor entrances from beneath the seating area onto the thrust. The forestage was widened and extended four feet to open up entrances and acting areas downstage of the penthouse columns. The side walls of the stage were widened to open the stage up to the audience, but the side stages became less used because they were blocked by the penthouse columns, scenery, and actors performing on platforming on the stage.

The introduction of post-seventeenth-century costuming in productions beginning in the 1970s also opened the door for the introduction of modern scenic design. At first costumes for a single production in the Elizabethan theatre might be set in the eighteenth or nineteenth centuries, but by the 1990s costumes as well as sets were modern or postmodern, and few productions used costumes prior to the seventeenth century.

As early as the 1960s attempts were already being made to cover the Tudor facade with curtains or decorations. There has been a progressive elaboration of the coverings. Sometimes extensive platforms and levels are set up in front of the pavilion and on the forestage. Most of the shows today extend at least one platform downstage of the pavilion or at an upper level of eight feet off the stage floor. A recent production of *The Taming of the Shrew* had a platform that reached to the stage-right casement window, and *Troilus and Cressida* used an "outer above" that was even lower than the pavilion and bridged between the penthouse columns and had two spiral staircases around the columns. Pipes, square steel tubes, or wooden frameworks have been set up on the main and side stages to support changeable or sliding curtains or panels for scenic effects.

Other uses of the Tudor facade have changed its nature. The facade becomes a "neutral" background or surround, like a cyclorama, behind the main-stage scenery. This can be accomplished in at least two ways. The first is by setting up visually stimulating sets in front of the pavilion and facade, which was done as early as 1970 in a production of *The Comedy of Errors*, when an architectural representation of a street with houses was set up in front of the Elizabethan facade. The second method is by focusing all of the light off the facade so that, by contrast, it disappears and becomes a "void" background.

Since 1991 there have been two more artistic directors and numerous directors and designers who are contracted for a show or two. Each of the directors and designers has attempted to put an individual stamp on the production. There is certainly a heated discussion between those who wish to "translate" Shakespeare for modern audiences and those who would like to see plays staged as they were traditionally and find the parallels with modern experience without changing Shakespeare into a modern playwright. As early as 1975 the Oregon Shakespearean Festival was having this discussion when Bowmer wrote:

> In Jon Jory's 1975 production of *All's Well That Ends Well* he used a curtain across the stage in front of the pavilion throughout the play. All entrances and exits are made through or around the ends of this curtain. This together with the use of Commedia mimes to effect the transitions simply denied the Elizabethan flavor which is so much a part of the Festival's tradition. . . . This very striking production could have been done on any stage. It is my firm belief that, aside from the essential fluidity it provides, the festival's Elizabethan stage, with its architectural façade provides an essential Renaissance overtone which must be recognized by directors who wish to continue our enviable tradition.[13]

Bowmer's dream of a modified Elizabethan stage survived many years past his own retirement, but during the last fifteen years the use of the stage for representative Renaissance productions has been eroded. Productions of *Romeo and Juliet* and *Coriolanus* during the 1996 season provide two of the most egregious examples of the misuse of the Elizabethan stage. The balcony scene in *Romeo* did not use the balcony at all, and Romeo and Juliet, in sort of modern dress, performed the scene writhing around on the main-stage floor unable to reach each other. The Elizabethan facade was covered by pipes hanging in front of it. The inner above was used rarely and not for any significant action with actors partially obscured by the pipes. *Coriolanus* used four construction scaffolds placed across the stage. Although they did not cover all of the facade, they certainly de-emphasized it since they were light-colored steel pipe. The "postmodern" production had the actors in a mix of military outfits from all periods—Roman to modern—and using both swords and machine guns. The costumes in *Love's Labor's Lost* the same season were eighteenth century, but the set was a series of stairs and structures in front of the facade. Subsequent seasons have featured the same kind of disregard for the architectural stage.

The Oregon Shakespeare Festival is not the only Elizabethan reproduction experiencing this kind of scenic "cover-up." The 2001 production of *King Lear* at the London Globe neutralized the stage facade by covering it with slats. Audiences in both theatres are disappointed—those at the Globe because they don't go to the Globe to see the kind of theatre you can see anywhere, according to Frank Hildy. Actor-director Jerry Turner, who was with the festival with Bowmer before becoming the second artistic director from 1971 to 1991, wrote that the continuity of people who worked at the Oregon Shakespeare Festival created "a unit that shares a lot of time and energy and joy with each other. . . . That there's a love affair here between the audience and the players is a fact that goes a long way toward the success of the place. They feel passionately about it! They own it! They can get *mad* about it."[14] This comment applies to an audience composed largely of loyal supporters and longtime members who return year after year. This is a passionate audience in Ashland; they know what they want to see and are vocal about it if it fails to please.

Even though there is space for experimentation with production styles for Shakespearean and other plays in the festival's two indoor theatres, there are some who have proposed that the Tudor facade be redesigned to remove any sort of historical references in order to achieve a neutral background as a sort of outdoor version of the Bowmer Theatre. Angus Bowmer's dream has turned into a nightmare for those who attend the festival to see Shakespeare and expect a Renaissance representation. Will the loyal audiences continue to support the current production practices, or will they simply age out and be replaced by younger audiences imbued with a tradition of pop culture? Current productions at the Oregon Shakespeare Festival are not meeting the expectations of Ashland's mature audiences, on whose patronage the continued success of the festival depends.

Since the opening of the Ashland Elizabethan Theatre in 1935, there have been many so-called Globe reproductions, including several in the United States in addition to the well-known one in London and new theatres in Prague, Rome, and Gdansk. However, the *current users* of these theatres are not always devoted to exploring or demonstrating the original practices of the early playhouses as a way toward understanding Shakespeare's plays. The idealistic builders of the hypothetical reconstructions may be disappointed to realize that most practitioners today chafe at the implied limitations of the architectural stage to production and interpretation and will try to impose modern concepts on the texts as well as visual images on these stages. These stages as built become an interesting novelty—a tourist attraction—rather than a way to help audiences understand the plays as Shakespeare conceived them.

Notes

1. Angus Bowmer, *Chapbook #1: Shreds and Patches: The Ashland Elizabethan Stage* (Ashland: Oregon Shakespearean Festival Association, 1978), 13.

2. Angus Bowmer, "Shakespeare in Ashland: 25 Years of Theatre," Oregon Shakespearean Festival Association program, 1965, 2–3.

3. The festival operated under this name until 1988, when the Oregon Shakespearean Festival shortened its official name slightly to the Oregon Shakespeare Festival.

4. Angus Bowmer, *As I Remember Adam* (Ashland: Oregon Shakespearean Festival Association, 1975), 159–60.

5. Remarks at Southeastern Theatre Conference, Arlington, VA, Mar. 8, 2003.

6. Angus Bowmer, *Chapbook #2: Shreds and Patches: Acting and Directing on the Ashland Elizabethan Stage* (Ashland: Oregon Shakespearean Festival Association, 1979), 16.

7. Photo archives, Oregon Shakespearean Festival Association.

8. "The Oregon Shakespeare Festival: Celebrating 60 Years," Oregon Shakespeare Festival program, 1995, 3.

9. Information about the physical stage and scenic practices is drawn from the Oregon Shakespeare Festival photo archives and personal experience of Richard L. Hay since 1952.

10. C. Walter Hodges, *The Globe Restored* (London: Ernest Benn, 1953), 59.

11. Oregon Shakespearean Festival program, 1956, 28.

12. "Celebrating 60 Years," 5.

13. Bowmer, "The Elizabethan Stage," 42.

14. "Celebrating 60 Years," 4.

Location as a Monumentalizing Factor at Original and Reconstructed Shakespearean Theatres

Johanna Schmitz

"YOU ARE HERE" is the simple caption on a popular poster sold in the Rose Theatre gift shop. The major components of the Rose presentation are depicted in the poster's image surrounded by the footprint of Rose Court, the modern building that stands over and frames the site. In the center are the ghostly faces of Shakespeare and Marlowe (a bit larger and brighter than Shakespeare's) staring up from beneath the illuminated Rose Theatre foundation, as if to suggest that by looking at the archaeological remains one might be looking into the face of genius.

So far, and perhaps ultimately, there are only two Elizabethan theatre archaeological sites identified, marked, and to some degree made accessible for the visitor and tourist in Bankside: the buried foundations of the Rose and the Globe theatres are situated almost directly opposite each other on Park Street. Although both participate in the commemorative activity surrounding Shakespeare's career, and indeed all Elizabethan theatre, they function as very different kinds of artifacts. The Globe is entombed and memorialized, whereas the Rose, which is marketed as the "first theatre in Bankside" and an "active archeological site," offered until recently a complex and evolving public exhibition (simple access to the space is still available by special request as part of the New Globe's super tour).

Although the Rose provides closer proximity to surviving foundations than are available at the original Globe, the visitor's experience does not provide visual confirmation of the theatre itself. The fragile archaeological remains have been covered over for their protection, and the visitor, drawn into the basement of Rose Court by the authenticated location

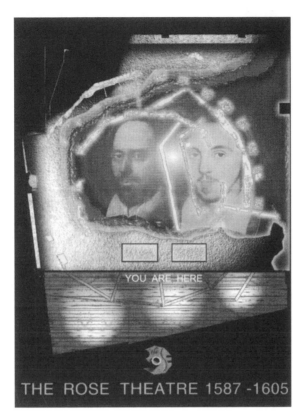

Rose Theatre poster. Designed by William Dudley. Used by permission of Rose Theatre Trust.

of the Rose, sees the surface of these protective layers of water, sand, and foundation markers, while being told, by guides and other educational materials, about the value of what lies just out of sight and what might be eventually exhumed. The commodity the visitors take away is that they have experienced the location of the Rose Theatre much like one might visit a gravesite.

The contribution of the Rose Theatre to current and future scholarship cannot be overstated. However, I have struggled to define the special value and impact of visiting the Rose location and will rely on a short statement from a Web site maintained by the University of Reading, where the Rose archives are held: "The Rose site has a remarkable 'tingle factor,' generated by its authenticity: visitors stand where Shakespeare stood, over the remains of a genuine Elizabethan theatre. This was what brought many leading members of the theatrical profession, and thousands of ordinary people, to rally to the site's defense in 1989."[1]

It is this notion of a "tingle factor," generated by visiting a location, that brings me to larger questions involving architectural reconstruction. When an original artifact has been lost, decays, or is too precious for presentation and/or use, is it possible for a newly created, distanced, and thereby recreated and artificial artifact to stand in for the inaccessible "real" one? What happens to the reception of such a reconstruction? For example, there is some question about whether the Crown Jewels on display in the Tower of London are the real royal jewels or copies. Would tourists be drawn to the site and stand in line to see them if the tourists knew the artifacts were simulated? It seems that artifacts, such as the jewels, are usually examined only as an extant part of their original context, as a separated survivor from an identifiable event or environment. The Theatre Museum in London, for example, is filled with displays of all sorts of things, from Ratty's boating jacket from the *Wind in the Willows* to Ellen Terry's shoes. Unlike these portable artifacts, location has the expectation of immersion, of the availability of spatial context, and cannot be transported in any way other than virtual recreation or simulation.

The audience for an architectural reconstruction understands of course that the building they enter is not the same building Shakespeare used but a facsimile and, hopefully, one that Shakespeare would recognize as a useable performance space. The question here is, how would the experience of a Rose reconstruction on the exact location of the original differ from the experience at a reconstruction built some distance away? Would some part of the spectacle in such a building be that the Titus Andronicus before this modern audience is standing exactly on the same spot where the first Titus stood; and, regardless of production aesthetics or playing practice, would the location of the actor contribute in some way to the authenticity of that performance?[2] Would the pressures and perception of authenticity be greater for such a building constructed exactly on top of authentic foundations than, say, for Shakespeare's Globe Theatre (or the New Globe), which is built near but not precisely on top of its original? Of course it would. One need only imagine Kathryn Hunter performing King Lear on some sort of reconstructed Globe over the original location on Park Street to see how the presence of a female actor would magnify the deviation from what we accept as historical authenticity to a greater degree than perceived at the Young Vic (1997). With architectural reconstructions of the Rose, Globe, and Blackfriars proliferating around the world from San Diego to Rome

Interior of Blackfriars Playhouse, Staunton, Virginia. Used by permission of Shenandoah Shakespeare. Photo by Lee Brauer.

(a reconstructed Globe opened in Rome's Villa Bourghese on October 14, 2003) it is important to ask what happens to the "tingle factor" of location offered by perceived proximity of the original London sites when reconstructions are undertaken so far away from their original location and imagined context. My concern here is to question how the location of the New Globe in Southwark, which opened its first full season in 1997 and is the first Shakespeare reconstruction to be tied so closely to its authentic setting, and the new Blackfriars Playhouse reconstruction, which opened, also with wide but very different acclaim, in Virginia in September of 2001, generate very different expectations for resurrection, authenticity, and receptive, commodified experience.

Although both the original Globe and Rose sites are subordinate to the New Globe in turning Bankside into a tourist destination, they also certainly contribute to the monumental status of the New Globe: they are relatively passive and static precursors studied as sources for physical evidence for the design and operation of the new theatre and, perhaps just as important, for pinpointing two of the primary locations of Elizabethan theatrical activity in Bankside. In previous work centered on the New Globe Theater in London I have defined a cultural monument as having (1) a shared acknowledgment or understanding of that which is commemorated (in this case Shakespeare) that attracts an audience or visitor, (2) a visible investment of resources (that is, financial, intellectual, natural, labor, and so forth), and (3) a marked physical location made accessible in order to acknowledge the event or undertaking that is being commemorated.[3] Architectural reconstructions provide such virtual environments in which an audience is given a physical experience as they access these new buildings, which, I argue, are, more than any other function, immersive monuments.

It is only after the rediscovery of the original Globe and Rose sites that the question and implication of "actual" and/or "authentic" location vs. new, or foreign, location has become an intriguing question with competing sites to consider. Inherent in the investigation is the special value given to place of origin vs. displaced location and the conflict between authenticated artifacts and those that are recreated. Because the Rose is an active archaeological site, which helped to inform the design and use of the New Globe, it simultaneously authorizes and antagonizes the legitimacy of the new structure. The New Globe, on the other hand, is a different kind of contemporary artifact as it presents a completed model extrapolated from available evidence and scholarly conjecture, as well as the desires of the resident artistic staff and, of course, government building requirements. It exists in a doubleness of doing and showing and "as then" and "now," and presents a tension between what was found and replicated vs. what is invented to complete the structure and the performances within it.

I have argued that the New Globe project, doggedly pursued for decades by Sam Wanamaker, was ultimately made possible in its present form only after popular and academic interest was generated by the archaeological discoveries of the Rose and Globe theatres in the late 1980s, as well as by the growing tourism trade, which is increasingly linked to the heritage industry based on offering authenticized experiences for cultural, recreational, and serious leisure tourists who may have either professional or nonworking careers in theatre or Shakespeare.[4] Since the discoveries of the original sites, however, these "actual" locations have been rendered inaccessible and silent, and their location and commodity as destination have been taken over and eclipsed by the New Globe.

The interesting twist here is that because the New Globe in many ways ignores the archaeological site at the same time that it depends on it for the value of legitimizing its location, the research, and the product of that research, has been turned on its head. The discovery of the original Globe and Rose sites, and the structural information gleaned from these digs, informed the design of the New Globe, but the entombment and invisibility of the original Globe also causes the visitors and audience to imagine the old Globe by viewing the new one. The reversal is that the New Globe informs the old one. The loss of the original determined the need for reconstruction, and the virtual experience at the New Globe shows what is lost at the old site. The New Globe also adds another layer of entombment over the original because the need to recover the decaying fragment has been further diminished.[5] The outcome has been, for better or worse, that masses "experience" the New Globe, and few visit, or "pay homage" to, the Old Globe and Rose sites.

The original is approximately three hundred feet southeast of the New Globe complex and lies several feet underground. It is located underneath Southwark Bridge Road (and its massive on/off ramp leading up to Southwark Bridge) and the Old Theatre Court (a new name for what was Anchor Terrace courtyard and apartments) on Park Street. The terrace's footprint, as wide as the bridge next to it, covers about half of the original Globe's foundations. The western fourth of the Globe is under Southwark Bridge Road. The remaining fourth lies under the new courtyard, which separates the old Anchor Terrace from a modern residential structure that mirrors it on the eastern end of the block. The only markers that indicate where the Globe is are some textured brick and stonework and a black granite slab with large metal letters set into the surface that read "The Globe" positioned approximately "over" the remains of the original theatre.

Visitors are prevented from walking into the courtyard by a tall black metal fence curved away from the sidewalk so that visitors can stop to ponder the site but also remain out of the foot traffic on Park Street. Just behind the fence to the left are three large informational reader boards that give a brief history of the site and of Elizabethan theatre in general. Other than these boards there is very little visual interest at the Old Globe site since the archaeology has been covered over. Other than the surface markers, the experience the site offers is limited to a memorialization of something buried and to the imagination of the distanced and passive visitor. Because the visual marker stands near the actual site of the building and because it communicates an irretrievable loss, the entire site is closer to a memorial or a tombstone than a cultural monument. As Peggy Phelan writes, "[a] tomb is appealing precisely because it is static and still, unlike the decomposing body it covers. . . . Architecture offers us this monumental stillness and helps transform dying into death."[6] The "architecture" that marks the stillness at the original Globe site includes the Anchor Terrace residential building and the specially designed educational reader boards and the black stone marker in the courtyard, visible from the sidewalk. I believe the site is appealing, however, even to serious leisure tourists, because of an intangible feeling, perhaps the "tingle factor" of proximity, that can be imagined when one is near the authentic and original location and fragments of the original theatre(s) that are promised to still be buried there.

Although monuments do not necessarily have to occupy space on or near the actual site of commemoration, the most powerful monuments often do. A monument associated with a physical space or destination offers a proximity to the commemorated that a distanced monument cannot. There are several kinds of cultural monuments (and memorials) that depend on the actuality of an identifiable place in order to generate an audience for that location; Civil War battlefields, national parks, and preserved houses of past presidents such as the Woodrow Wilson house in Staunton, Virginia, near the new Blackfriars Playhouse are examples of such monuments. One of the key contributions of the artifact of the original Globe to the reconstruction located just around the block is that it authorizes theatrical activity in this specific location and offers a memorial experience. As Barbara Kirshenblatt-Gimblett wrote in *Destination Culture*: "[Such markers] assert 'hereness,' an immediacy to the commemorated that is achieved when some event or undertaking is localized to a particular identifiable site. It is this 'hereness' that is necessary to 'convert a location to a destination.'"[7] I would add that this "hereness" falsely seems to make time the only separation between the event or undertaking and the visitor:

> Tourists travel to actual destinations to experience virtual places. They set out for the very spot where the Pilgrims of Plimoth Plantation once lived, the foundations from whence the Abby Church of Saint Peter and Saint Paul in Cluny once rose, the Registry Hall where immigrants traveling steerage to America once stood, only to find that the actual spot is remarkably mute. Hence, the need for a re-created Pilgrim village, computer simulation of the reconstructed church, and restoration and interpretation of Ellis Island.[8]

Tourists seek out the New Globe partly for the same reason. They seek authenticity and are given a reconstruction that marks the authentic location with an accessible physical destination. When considering the monumental nature of the location and the structure, it is interesting to note that more people take the guided tour of the building than see a play there. Indeed, location is key to the magnetism of the building, and the New Globe capitalizes on its (nearly) authentic location even though it purposefully lacks authentic artifacts within it (except for old books for sale in the gift shop). The proximity of the building to the original site and the magnificence of the structure and its visual authority cause a prevalent confusion among the public (partially ignored, some would say supported, by the New Globe) about whether the New Globe stands exactly on the site of the original. Indeed, many of the publications generated by the Globe have purposefully confused the locations of the original and new theatres, often conflating the original Globe with the new one. One reads: "Now, the fully reconstructed Globe Theatre is once again open on the south bank of the Thames, just as it was when Shakespeare's greatest plays were first presented there." And another: "To Americans who care about the splendors of their language, the great tradition of classic drama and the preservation of a singularly historic building, membership in the American Friends [of the Globe] is an honor; a pleasure and a way to demonstrate their interest and concern." A third example of this marketing technique is that the summer of 1999 was called the New Globe's Anniversary Season, marking the four-hundredth anniversary of the theatre. The recreated heritage of the building was also reinforced by a poster for the Globe Theatre performance season with the following caption implying a continuous lineage from the first Globe to the new one: "First Globe: 1599, Second Globe 1614, Third Globe 1997."[9]

Although this confusion over actual, or nearly actual, location is significant when considering how the presentation of the site is received, there are other factors that contribute to the magnetism of the complex. One of the many attractions other than "hereness" is that the New Globe offers a unique, singularly dedicated, Shakespeare site in London. It is interesting that London, increasingly dependent on its tourism industry, did not find a way to compete with Stratford-upon-Avon for locations marking England's most famous cultural commodity before 1997. Although it is true that Shakespeare was commemorated in London with statues and other markers, and his plays were continually produced, in some form or another, until the New Globe began construction in the early 1990s, London had no destination solely dedicated to commemorating Shakespeare or Shakespeare's theatre.

In retrospect, the pairing of the monument of the New Globe with the location of the historical activity is now so obvious that it is indeed surprising that the value of the location was not marked and visibly acknowledged in some more prominent way before Wanamaker "discovered" and was motivated by the bronze plaque in 1946 that marked the general area. Perhaps Garrick's Stratford Jubilee of 1769, the catalyst for making Stratford England's primary Shakespeare destination, had already fulfilled the need and the market for a Shakespeare location linked to authentic sites: Anne Hathaway's Cottage, Hall's Croft, and, of course, Holy Trinity, where Shakespeare's bones still warn would-be thieves to leave him alone. Certainly, because Shakespeare was born, retired, and is buried there, most of the town can be said to be an authentic Shakespeare location; and until the New Globe was completed, Stratford, not London, had been the primary Shakespeare destination in England. The magnitude of the New Globe and its surrounding complex, however, causes it to be ranked a close second to Stratford in the market for cultural tourists. Some might argue that this completely new building has in fact replaced Shakespeare's Stratford as the primary site for visiting Shakespeare's legacy because of the active immersive experience it offers.

The New Globe's visible investment of resources, attraction of a massive and international audience, and its valuable and nearly authentic location cause it to be used, presented, received, and supported in a very different way from theatre reconstructions undertaken in foreign locations, which are distanced from the location of their Elizabethan and Jacobean theatrical past. Like the New Globe, the new Blackfriars Playhouse also enjoys and endures the magnetism generated by historical reconstruction as it draws people to Staunton, Virginia, to see and experience the unusual playing space and the performance that happens there. Unlike reconstruction of the Globe and Rose archaeological site in London, however, its location isolates the new building and reduces the auxiliary pressures of participating in the interpretation of the original Blackfriars Playhouse location and the historical context of Shakespeare's London. What is less obvious is how this decontextualization affects the use, mission, marketing plan, and reception of the building. In other words, one might ask, what happens to the "tingle factor" so far from Southwark (and Stratford), and how will this distance affect the way in which the theatre is used and the project received?

I imagine that the physical distance of the new Blackfriars Playhouse not only diminishes the monumental pressures of the building and the performance within it but also allows a closer connection to the "test kitchen" aspects of such a reconstruction. In blatant terms, because it is Shakespeare's other playhouse, because it is located in America, because there is no active archaeology at the original site, and because Americans are the primary administrators and performers (no small point to my friends in London), could there be less of a popular expectation for historical "authenticity" and a higher tolerance for experimentation and receptive authenticity, the sort of authenticity so sought out by Mark Rylance, the artistic director at the New Globe?[10] Certainly its location will draw a different audience, but does its location cause it therefore to enjoy less authority? Can it be dismissed as merely an American experiment?

Location is not the only difference that impacts the activity at the reconstructions I have mentioned here, but it is one of the most significant factors in how these reconstructions are presented and perceived. In addition to the relative celebrity of the New Globe vs. the lesser-known Blackfriars, the design choices made to meet current popular expectation for Elizabethan architecture (as well as to adhere to current building codes), the makeup of the playing companies and the different scope of the education plans at the two structures, and the simple configuration of one space as an amphitheatre and the other as an enclosed interior are just some of the other key components worthy of scholarly attention. For example, academic circles have discussed that the New Globe has made concessions, especially in design elements, to what its international audience has imagined to be, and is prepared to accept as, Elizabethan or "Shakespearean." In what way will the separation from the authority of the original site, and the fact that the Blackfriars Playhouse is Shakespeare's lesser-known theatre, cause this expectation of "authenticity" to be met or thwarted at the new Blackfriars Playhouse? Because there is less of a preconceived popular expectation at the new Blackfriars Playhouse, could it have more authority as it provides the first popular model of this playhouse (unlike the New Globe in London)? Certainly the administrators do not hope to attract the numbers to Staunton that Stratford or the New Globe do in England. In what way does location contribute to the kind of audience it will develop? Can it develop tourism interested in the building and not the performance within it?

All future reconstructions will also struggle with the fact that they are endeavoring to recreate a theatre for a lost performance practice to serve an audience unaccustomed to, and at the same time enthralled by, the unique spatial and visual environment of an Elizabethan playhouse. Of course, authenticity becomes a measure by which any reconstruction of heritage is judged. Whether the authenticity is recreated (as in the case of all of these reconstructions of the Elizabethan playhouses) or is attributed to an artifact that is then framed and presented in a museum setting, authenticity offers its audience a link, a piece of proof, indicating that the larger picture is only lost to us through the passing of time and memory. The reconstructionist hopes that by piecing together enough of the authentic, or authenticized, fragments, the larger picture will reappear and that we will be able to figure out how to use these recreated tools to discover a recreated experience. In this way each reconstruction demonstrates the desire to recover a proximity to "Shakespeare" and a version of culture and heritage. How "authentic location" enables or inhibits these endeavors is something I will continue to try to figure out. This project might include a consideration of practice or artifact that is tied to location but can travel away from that location: British actors with British accents is one example that comes to mind; companies, like Patrick Tucker's, that endeavor to recreate original playing practice might be another. The buildings themselves continue to be the most concrete artifact to shape the performances within them, but their impact on contemporary Shakespeare production and reception is an issue that clearly craves more scholarly and practical attention.

There are other reconstruction projects under way that will augment the discussion of recreated playing spaces in distanced locations, including a New Globe in Rome; a New Rose by Shakespeare and Company in Lennox, Massachusetts; and a second Globe also in Staunton, Virginia. The negotiation between what kinds of artifacts scholars and practitioners think might be authentic and what the audience expects to see, and/or is willing to accept, is the ongoing project of Elizabethanists and reconstructionists alike. I look forward to many immersive experiences, wherever they may be located, as the quest to recreate Shakespeare's theatres continues.

Notes

1. Rose Theatre Trust, Rose Theatre Exhibition, Aug. 15, 2003, http://www.rosetheatre.org.uk (accessed Oct. 20, 2003).

2. The Royal Shakespeare Company performed a reading of *Titus Andronicus* at the Rose site to benefit the Rose Theatre Trust on August 31, 2003.

3. Johanna Schmitz, "Desire for Authenticity: Millennial Reconstructions of Shakespeare's Theater" (PhD diss., University of California–Davis, 2001).

4. Ibid., 77–81.

5. The fact that there is another archaeological site across the street also diminishes the need to uncover the Globe because similar, if not almost identical, building techniques and materials can be examined at the Rose excavation.

6. See Peggy Phelan, "Uncovered Rectums: Disinterring the Rose Theatre," in her *Mourning Sex: Performing Public Memories* (London: Routledge, 1997), 83.

7. Barbara Kirshenblatt-Gimblett, *Destination Culture: Tourism, Museums, and Heritage* (Berkeley: University of California Press, 1998), 7.

8. Ibid., 9.

9. American Friends of Shakespeare's Globe membership brochure, July

1997; International Shakespeare Globe Center, Globe USA membership brochure, July 1997; Shakespeare's Globe Theatre, Education Office, Globelink poster, Aug. 1997.

10. Receptive authenticity differs from antiquarian authenticity in that the former endeavors to recreate an authentic experience rather than a historical recreation of playing practice and artifact.

Why Elizabethan Spaces?

Franklin J. Hildy

SINCE MY DAYS AS A graduate student at Northwestern University I have been fascinated by theatre architecture. I have always wanted to know what accounted for the fact that some theatre spaces are able to bring the very best out of even the most pedestrian of productions, whereas other theatre spaces can crush the life out of the most spirited of performances. My attempts to find some possible answers have led me to a lifelong interest in the ways theatre architecture influences audience experience. At a time when my colleagues were concerned almost exclusively with the much lauded actor/audience relationship, I was concerned with both that and the relationship the architecture allowed the audience to have with itself or, perhaps more precisely, the way architecture influenced the relationship the various components of that social grouping we call "an audience" could have with each other. Good theatre spaces facilitate the successful interchange of energy between actors and audience, but they also facilitate the generation of energy within the audience itself. In my early work as a theatre consultant I gained a good deal of practical experience in understanding some of the dynamics of this interchange of energy. But I soon realized that to attempt any reasonable speculation about what made a successful theatre, I needed to explore successful theatres of the past. So I set myself the task of looking at all of the existing theatres that were originally built before 1800 and at a good sampling of the most successful theatres to have been built since. This exploration has taken me from Sweden to Turkey and from Japan to Malta. It has also given me the opportunity to explore in great detail theatres from the Roman Odeon at Nikopolis in Greece, to the Corral de Comedias at Almagro in Spain

(1628) to the Cesky Kromlov palace theatre in the Czech Republic (1766).

There are numerous lessons to be learned from the study of historic theatre buildings. I like to refer to this work as "applied theatre history" because of its implications for modern theatre. Among those lessons that seem most relevant to the topic at hand are three maxims I have developed for modern theatre architects.

Maxim one. There is no place for dead space in the live theatre. Wherever one looks in a historic theatre auditorium there are signs of life or the potential for life. Within each audience member's range of vision, while watching a play in a historic theatre, there are other audience members or at least fake boxes that suggest the possibility that other audience members could be found there. Even doors like those found in Wagner's famous Festspielhouse in Bayreuth can suggest the potential for life to arrive at any moment. In places where the architecture does not allow for such features in a historic theatre, there are statues or paintings or some other signs of life virtually everywhere that might catch a playgoer's eye. To neutralize a space in order to put focus on the stage is to miss the point of what live theatre is all about.

Maxim two. Black is not a color that should ever be found in the audience space of a theatre. Theatres must have the ability to become psychologically "warm "or "cool" spaces depending on the drama being presented. You never see black in the original color scheme of a historic theatre because black can never be a warm color.

Maxim three. The space occupied by an audience during performance is known as "the house" to theatre people—there is a reason for that! Admittedly this is a less tangible lesson and one I have yet to fully understand. But there is something about successful theatre spaces that makes each member of the audience feel psychologically comfortable as soon as he or she enters, no matter how opulent or Spartan the interior decoration scheme might be and no matter how physically comfortable or uncomfortable the audience seating might be. How this feeling is conveyed to an audience is one of the greater mysteries of successful theatre architecture. But labeling this space as the "auditorium" on an architectural plan may well prevent an architect from giving the proper amount of thought to that mystery.

As with all historic research, there are limitations to the kind of exploration I do into historic theatres. In approaching the topic of our symposium, "Elizabethan Performance in North American Spaces," two of those limitations struck me as particularly cogent. First, focusing on just the concept of "performance in spaces," I note that it is rare to be able to study a historic theatre "in performance," that is, while a play is going on within it. On those occasions when performances are done in a historic theatre, however, it is remarkable how even a modern audience, one that cannot see with the same eyes as the audience for which the theatre was originally built, still experiences the energy interchange that is such an essential characteristic of a successful theatre building. Our symposium topic also calls attention to the fact that some of the most successful theatre architecture ever created was created in London when Elizabethan plays were being written. But none of those unique structures survived the turbulent middle years of the seventeenth century, so no examples of those remarkable theatres have come down to us. Holding this symposium in Staunton, Virginia, home of Shenandoah Shakespeare's reconstructed Blackfriars Playhouse (1608), is a powerful reminder that for more than one hundred years theatre people in North America have tried to make up for the loss of those Elizabethan spaces by reconstructing them, or perhaps a better term might be "recreating" them.

There has been an almost unbroken tradition of recreating Elizabethan theatrical spaces in North America since at least 1897. I became part of that tradition in 1984 when I joined the American-born actor/director Sam Wanamaker's project to rebuild the first Globe (1599) near its original site in London, a project inspired by American reconstructions and primarily funded through its first twenty-five years with money raised in the United States. I am part of the group working on a reconstruction of the second Globe (1614), intended to join the Blackfriars in Staunton, and on the reconstruction of the first Rose playhouse (1587) for Shakespeare and Company in Lenox, Massachusetts. Over the years I have been involved with numerous other reconstruction projects, some still pending and many abandoned long ago. I track numerous other such projects around the world as director of the Shakespeare Globe Center USA Research Archive, and I am fully aware that the desire to rebuild these particular lost theatres goes way beyond any general interest in theatre architecture. Why Elizabethan spaces? In reviewing the history of the attempt to reconstruct them, I believe some answers will become clear.

As the title of our symposium suggests, Elizabethan plays can be, and certainly have been, done in every kind of North American space. Some of the most interesting experiments with the performance of Elizabethan plays in North America, however, have been done in spaces that were intended to be recreations of Elizabethan spaces. Since most of this work was focused around the production of Shakespeare's plays, it is going to be necessary to look at the stage history of those plays in order to put this work into context. Studies of Shakespeare's quartos and folios suggest that the texts of his plays were altered, even in his own lifetime, for a variety of reasons.[1] They were altered for touring or for private performances, they were altered to accommodate changes in the membership of the acting companies, and they were altered just to make them fresher for revival. (And this is to say nothing about the way they were altered during the printing process.) The same was undoubtedly true for all successful plays in Shakespeare's day. During the commonwealth period some of Shakespeare's texts were edited down to mere comic sketches or "drolls." In the Restoration the plays were altered, adapted, and improved to fit contemporary tastes. William Davenant, who liked to encourage the rumor that he was Shakespeare's illegitimate son, for example, made *The Tempest* (1667) into an extravaganza with a multitude of added characters. John Dryden demonstrated how Shakespeare should have written *Antony and Cleopatra* with his play *All for Love* (1677), and Nahum Tate "fixed" *King Lear* (1681) to make it more suitable to modern tastes—the list could go on and on.[2] Such treatment of Shakespeare's plays was the norm for more than 150 years. When viewed in this context our own tendency to update, refocus, or otherwise alter the texts of Shakespeare's plays seems far more traditionalist than innovative.

But even in these early years, when professionals performed any one of his plays "as they liked it," the scripts themselves were going through editions by Rowe (1709), Pope (1725), and Theobald (1733).[3] These editors were attempting to save the texts that had been printed in Shakespeare's day, or at least printed by those who actually knew Shakespeare. They were not above "correcting" the texts that had come down to them in their attempts to regularize the plays for a reading public,[4] but their efforts stimulated an interest in the notion of an "authentic" text. They also stimulated an interest in the idea that it would be worth seeing these "authentic" texts onstage. In 1737 those with such an interest got their first chance when Covent Garden staged a relatively unaltered version of the Folio text of *Much Ado about Nothing*. This was a pioneering production in the long struggle to perform Shakespeare's plays using a text as it had been printed during the age that had first seen Shakespeare's plays produced.[5] Soon this notion was being championed by David Garrick, and although it cannot be said that he himself ever acted in a fully restored text of a Shakespeare play, his advocacy for the cause certainly accelerated the trend, especially after his production of *Macbeth* in 1744.

Following hard on the heels of this growing interest in authentic texts was another important development, "pictorial illustration" onstage, sometimes referred to as "antiquarianism." Since Shakespeare's day it had been the practice to costume plays in modern stage dress, generally a heightened form of what audience members might see on the streets around them. Since the Restoration it was also the practice to stage these plays using stock perspective scenery. But in 1773 Charles Macklin costumed the main characters in his production of *Macbeth* in dress that was intended to illustrate the period of the story. This was quite a departure from standard practice, and it was duplicated only sporadically. In 1824, however, Charles Kemble took the next step in staging *King John* in full period costume with full period settings. But it was not until William Charles Macready took over the management of Covent Garden in 1837 that the use of "authentic" texts in combination with "historic costumes" became the vogue for Shakespearean productions. Only a few companies could afford to fully follow this fashion, but it gradually became a standard to which most companies aspired. It also became the nemesis of those who were creating what came to be known as "the Elizabethan Revival," the movement that would ultimately be responsible for the reconstruction of Elizabethan playing spaces in North America.

Almost as soon as the "antiquarian" approach to the staging of Shakespearean plays became popular, there were those who rebelled against it. Just as the Pre-Raphaelites in painting set themselves in opposition to the materialist art of the Industrial Revolution, there were those in the theatre who set themselves in opposition to pictorial illustration. Some opposed pictorial illustration because they could not afford it. Others opposed it because the logic of using authentic versions of the texts suggested the use of authentic staging practices as well. For them the historical accuracy they wanted to see in performance needed to come from the period in which the play text was written, not the period in which the play's story was set. Whereas the Pre-Raphaelites idealized what they saw as the purer vision of Gothic and early Renaissance art, those who rebelled against pictorial illustration in theatre saw this same purity in the performance styles that had existed in Europe prior to the advent of the proscenium-arch stage. Just as the early editors of Shakespeare's plays had provided the impetus for the investigation of "authentic" texts, later editors, this time Edward Capell (1767) and Edmond Malone (1790), provided the impetus (and the information) to undertake an exploration of original staging practices. The earliest actual experiments along these lines were by the German producers Ludwig Tieck and Karl Immermann, who began working on recovery of Elizabethan staging practices between 1836 and 1843. The first producer to take up this kind of experimentation in England was Benjamin

Webster, who staged *The Taming of the Shrew* "in its original form" at London's Haymarket Theatre in 1844. For this production, designed by J. R. Planché, "a couple of screens and a curtain, divided in the middle, form a veil to hide the actors off the stage, and labels affixed to the curtain denote the changes of scene," according to the *Athenaeum* (March 23, 1844). But the reviews were mixed on this "feature of novelty," and although the production was revived in 1847, it did not inspire any immediate imitators.

It was not until 1881 that the twenty-nine-year-old actor-manager William Poel took up the challenge of rediscovering Shakespearean staging practices with a production of *Hamlet* on a "draped stage" using the First Quarto text (with no additions from the Folio). As Robert Speaight has noted, this production can be said to be historic in that it was Poel's first effort.[6] But it is clear that Poel did not become a significant figure until after 1887, when he became an instructor for the Shakespeare Reading Society. In 1888 the famous de Witt drawing of the interior of the Swan Playhouse was discovered, the first and still the only contemporary view we have of the interior of any Elizabethan open-air theatre. Two years later Poel saw the Jocza Savits production of *King Lear* (1890) at the Munich Shakespeare theatre, presented on a stage designed for the production of classical plays.[7] The Swan drawing discovery and the Savits production reminded Poel that his own work was lacking the appropriate stage environment.[8] So in 1893 he introduced his "Fortune fit-up," on which to stage his production of *Measure for Measure* at the Royalty Theatre in London. Fit-ups were common touring stages during the Victorian era, designed to be erected in halls, and sometimes even in theatres, across the country. Poel called this one the "Fortune fit-up" to give it the authority of the Fortune contract, the most highly regarded document relating to Elizabethan theatre buildings. This fit-up was actually based, however, on the far less accepted Swan drawing, with numerous concessions made to the need for fit-ups to be adaptable to halls of all kinds. The Fortune fit-up stage was only 30 feet wide by 24 feet deep, substantially smaller than the 43 feet of width called for by the Fortune contract and the 27½ feet depth the contract is generally thought to imply.[9] Stage columns divided the stage depth in half, and the space behind the columns was further broken up by the small discovery space and balcony that occupied the last five feet of the stage area. In the following year Poel created the Elizabethan Stage Society, for which he produced plays from 1895 to 1905, and it was for this work, especially those productions that used the Fortune fit-up, that he became widely known.[10]

Poel's work in the recovery of the original staging practices for Shakespeare's plays and his influence on English theatre have been well documented. His influence on the French stage through the work of Aurélien Lugné-Poë, André Antoine, Jacques Copeau, and others has been less widely understood.[11] What is important to note here, however, is that Poel, and those who followed him, thought of themselves as members of the avant-garde. As early as 1877 the French critic Théodore de Banville had pleaded for a new theatre "where a single action continues without interruption in quite different locales."[12] This was exactly what Poel believed Shakespearean stagecraft had done. "Some people have called me an archaeologist," he told the *Daily Chronicle* in 1913, "but I am not. I am really a modernist. My original aim was just to find out some means of acting Shakespeare naturally and appealingly from the full text as in a modern drama."[13] Poel came to believe that the only means to this end was a return to the staging conventions used in Shakespeare's own day. The argument he developed over many years might best be summarized in this way. A playwright crafts plays just as a shipwright crafts ships. The conditions of performance that exist when a playwright is crafting a play help to give that play its form. If we are going to fully understand how a play works, we have to understand the conditions under which it was wrought for performance. Many people were attracted to this notion because they naively thought it would provide new insights into Shakespeare. Others were attracted by the validation this historic work could give to the growing movement toward simplified staging that would eventually become known as the "New Stagecraft." Poel was not the only one to advocate such ideas, and not all those who argued along these lines got their ideas from him.[14] But Poel was the most outspoken of them all, and when it comes to the actual reconstruction of Elizabethan spaces, he was the most influential.

Poel never wrote down what he considered the essential components of Shakespearean production methods, but one of his most distinguished followers, Sir Lewis Casson, did:

1. The full text in its proper order without interpolations or rearrangement.

2. Continuity of speech from scene to scene without breaks between "acts."

3. A permanent architectural set with at least two levels, and an inner stage covered by traverse curtains.

4. A wide platform stage projecting into the audience.

5.   Elizabethan dress (with a few period modifications).

6.   Rapid, highly coloured, musical speech, of great range and flexibility.[15]

Poel's advocacy for the full text in its proper order was not original, and Poel himself rarely practiced what he preached in this regard.[16] When it came to the continuity of speech and its rapid, highly colored delivery, Poel became increasingly preoccupied with a characteristically eccentric system he called "tones," which marred many of his own productions. B. Iden Payne describes this as a system in which the actors were "to speak all the unaccented words with great rapidity and staccato and to draw out the stressed word in a slow emphasis, with heavy inflection and with punctuation ignored."[17] So it was largely up to people like Harley Granville-Barker, Nugent Monck, W. Bridges-Adams, Robert Atkins, Harcourt Williams, Lewis Casson, B. Iden Payne, Thomas Wood Stevens, and Tyrone Guthrie to make the approach Poel advocated actually work successfully in performance (and it was the latter three who brought these practices to North America). Through them, continuity of action, the use of a permanent architectural set, and above all the use of the thrust stage became the new vogue in the staging of Shakespeare's plays, and they never failed to credit Poel with the original inspiration. As Guthrie said of Poel: "I believe that he, if anybody, ought to be regarded as the founder of modern Shakespearean production."[18] Certainly the thrust stages we find in many of our theatres today exist largely because of Poel's demonstration of their potential. Poel's advocacy for the use of Elizabethan costume, on the other hand, failed to achieve quite the same level of acceptance (although it was widely used, especially in America). Where the other components of his theories both saved money and fit in with the New Stagecraft agenda, Elizabethan dress was expensive. After Barry Jackson had success with his modern-dress productions of Shakespeare between 1923 and 1929, there was also a clear alternative approach to costuming that was both less costly and more trendy.

As they were passed down to Casson and others, Poel's essential components for the revival of authentic staging practices from Shakespeare's day included only an Elizabethan stage, not the rest of the building. But Poel was certainly aware that to get at the heart of Shakespeare's stagecraft, he needed to get beyond his "Fortune fit-up" stage; he needed an entire playhouse. In 1897 he made a drawing of what such a building might look like,[19] and by 1902 Poel's drawing had been converted to a model, the full-scale construction of which was the goal of the London Shakespeare Commemoration League. But that group metamorphosed into the Shakespeare Memorial National Theatre Committee in 1908 and eventually into the National Theatre Committee that built a quite un-Shakespearean National Theatre on the south side of the Thames in 1976.[20] Poel's proposal, meanwhile, was taken up by Mrs. George Cornwallis West, the former Lady Randolph Churchill, who was the American-born Jennie Jerome, mother of Winston Churchill. She persuaded the preeminent Edwardian architect Edwin Lutyens to create a full-scale Globe based on Poel's model, as part of the "Shakespeare's England" exhibition on the grounds of Earls Court in 1912.[21] This project was intended to raise money to build the proposed national theatre in time for Shakespeare's Tercentenary in 1916, but by the time that date arrived, all of Europe was distracted by the horrors of the Great War.

Poel went to the United States in 1916 to revive his London production of Ben Jonson's *Poetaster* at the Carnegie Institute of Technology, where the first degree-granting Department of Dramatic Arts in the world had been founded by Thomas Wood Stevens two years before.[22] Stevens did not initiate this program; it was the inspiration of the institute's president, Arthur Hammershlag, and its dean of the School of Applied Design, Russell Hewlett, but Stevens designed it and ran it for ten years. By the time he left Carnegie Tech, Stevens had succeeded in getting the professional theatre to accept that theatre could be taught in a college curriculum. One of the ways he did this was by hiring professional directors, like the expatriate English director B. Iden Payne, to teach regularly at the institute. As the first director of the Manchester Repertory Theatre in England, Payne had sponsored Poel's 1908 production of *Measure for Measure* and directed Poel in a production of *The Cloister* there in 1910. By his own admission he thought Poel's work with the Elizabethan stage a mere "passing curiosity,"[23] but like so many others he saw the potential in what Poel was doing for reinvigorating modern productions of Shakespeare's plays. Stevens saw this too, and eventually he and Payne developed "modified Elizabethan staging," an approach that was to revolutionize the production of Shakespeare's plays in America.[24]

By the time of Poel's arrival at Carnegie Tech, the United States had already taken the lead in the work being done on the reconstructing of Elizabethan theatre spaces. In 1895, just two years after Poel's Fortune fit-up in London, Harvard University built an Elizabethan stage for a production of Jonson's *Epicoene* in the 1,166-seat Sanders Theatre, which had been built in Memorial Hall in 1875. In 1904 George Pierce Baker had that stage redone by H. Langford Warren of the Architecture Department. They produced *Hamlet* there, with a professional company headed by Johnston Forbes-Robertson. Fifty Harvard students served as an Elizabethan audience in the "yard" (where they seem to have stood) and in the stage boxes. The Sanders Theatre was a "hall for academic occasions" modeled after the Sheldonian Theatre of 1668 in Oxford. It had three levels of galleries that came right up to the side of the stage, making it easily reconfigurable into something closely approximating an Elizabethan indoor playhouse. The open space between the galleries measured forty-seven feet across, just eight feet less than the yard at the Fortune Playhouse of 1600. This allowed them to construct a stage that was forty feet wide, ten feet wider than Poel's Fortune fit-up had been, and twenty feet deep, five feet shallower than the stage Poel had used. Poel had built a stage to test his own theories of Elizabethan staging, but for Baker this was an experiment to test competing theories of what the Elizabethan stages might have looked like and how they were most likely used.[25] In the year following this production the important American scholar G. F. Reynolds published his University of Chicago dissertation, "Some Principles of Elizabethan Staging," and the year after that the great American archival researcher C. H. Wallace finished his dissertation on the boys' company at the Blackfriars Playhouse (done at Freiburg University in Germany). In 1907 Baker published *The Development of Shakespeare as a Dramatist*—before going on to organize the famous "47 Workshop" (1912) and create the Yale School of Drama (1925). These men were soon joined in the quest to understand Elizabethan theatres by V. E. Albright (1909), T. S. Graves (1911), J. Q. Adams (1911), and A. H. Thorndike (1916), just to name the most prominent. Herbert Berry has observed that when it comes to the study of Elizabethan theatre, by 1917 the generally accepted "conception of the stage and the methods for producing plays on it was to a significant extent American."[26] Baker was certainly quick to point out that the 1895 and 1904 Harvard reconstructions had not been influenced by Poel's Fortune fit-up but had been independently arrived at.[27] The Harvard stage does show some remarkable similarities to Poel's fit-up, but that was almost inevitable given the nature of the available evidence. Baker's experience with staging was nowhere near that of Poel's, but the Harvard stage was supported by far more rigorous scholarship than anything Poel had been able to manage. Baker, for example, had two students comb through the stage directions of more than two hundred Elizabethan plays in an attempt to determine what was actually required for their performance.

Although the influence of American scholars grew through the 1920s, actual physical reconstructions were done elsewhere. In 1921 W. Nugent

Monck built the Maddermarket Theatre in Norwich, England, the first permanent theatre in that country to attempt to reproduce the conditions of an Elizabethan indoor theatre. Monck had acted in Poel's famous revival of *Everyman* in 1902 and served as Poel's most consistent stage manager from 1902 to 1908. He was soon recognized as a director who was more successful in the application of Poel's theories than Poel was himself. After its opening in 1921 the Maddermarket, therefore, quickly became a destination theatre for a veritable who's who of famous English directors, who came to see the work Monck did there and often "borrowed" his ideas. In 1933 Monck became the first director known to have personally staged all the plays in the Shakespeare canon, and Poel's ideas had been at the heart of all of them.[28] In the meantime the first permanent reconstruction of an Elizabethan outdoor theatre, or at least the stage end of one, was undertaken by "The Tsubouchi Memorial Theatre Museum," at Waseda University, Tokyo, in 1928. It was based on the well-known Walter H. Godfrey and William Archer model of the Fortune playhouse (1907), and the stage served as the front porch and entranceway to the museum. Both the Maddermarket and the Waseda Fortune still exist today, but it was the design of the Maddermarket that had the greatest impact on American theatres as it appears to have been the basis for the Elizabethan theatre designed by Paul Philippe Cret for the Folger Shakespeare Library in 1932. Both the Maddermarket and the Folger stages were influenced by the Archer/ Godfrey model of 1907, but the Maddermarket had added an extra door on each side of the stage, and the Folger Elizabethan theatre copied this eleven years later.[29]

Thomas Wood Stevens left Carnegie Tech in 1924, turned over the chairmanship of the Department of Dramatic Arts to B. Iden Payne, and moved to Chicago, where he became the founding director of the Goodman Theatre, one of the great regional theatres in the country. Two years later Payne joined him there. Stevens ran the Goodman until 1930, then embarked on a career as a freelance director. He had always been in demand as a director of pageants, had directed much of the best of world drama on the professional stage of the Goodman, and had the most impeccable credentials it was possible to have in academic theatre at that time. So in 1933, when Chicago celebrated its first hundred years as a city with "A Century of Progress: International Exhibition," it made sense for them to call on Stevens to help solve a problem. During the first season, it seems, those attending the exhibition had found it too unrelentingly futuristic and expressed an interest in something more traditional. One of the proposed exhibitions for 1934 was "Merry England," an enclosed village that would celebrate traditional English culture, largely through recreations of historic buildings. Stevens was asked to provide the entertainment for this village. Having been experimenting with Poel's ideas for some time, and perhaps having heard of the success of the 1912 Globe at Earls Court in London, Stevens proposed a Globe Theatre for the village, and one was soon designed to Stevens's specifications by Chicago architect Henry Hoskins. The design Stevens and Hoskins came up with stretched the eighty-foot square, described in the Fortune contract, into an elongated octagon fifty-five feet wide by seventy feet long (it was thirty-two feet high). The exterior side facing the "village square" was designed to make the building look round, and the opposite side, out of view of the public, was left polygonal. Inside was a yard that measured just thirty-six feet by forty-two feet, surrounded by three levels of galleries, the upper one of which was fake. The stage was small but shaped remarkably like those discovered in the Rose excavations of 1989. It thrust out sixteen feet into the audience (the first Rose stage thrust out about 16 feet, 5 inches). It measured only sixteen feet across the front (the first Rose stage measured close to twenty-seven feet) and tapered out to twenty-five feet where it intersected the frame (the Rose was nearly thirty-seven feet at that point). Both stages then tapered back along the lines of the frame so that the back of the stage was not as wide as the front. We do not know what was inside the frame at the Rose along the back of the stage, but Stevens and Hoskins put a discovery space measuring 14 feet wide by 7½ feet deep there, surmounted by a similarly sized balcony, just as Poel had always done.[30] By making the theatre so small—it seated just over four hundred—they lost the opportunity to achieve the kind of critical mass of audience needed to make the dynamics of Elizabethan theatre architecture work. By not having a third gallery audience, they unknowingly removed one of the key components of such a space. By seating the audience in the yard they prevented the space from generating the kind of energy and excitement we now know these buildings were capable of producing. And by elongating the shape they made the space as frontal as if they had simply used a standard auditorium with a balcony. The addition of a roof over the yard was also a major drawback to the authenticity they claimed for this building. The 1934 Globe reconstruction, then, was in many ways a step backward from the spaces designed for Harvard in 1895, but in spite of these failings more than four hundred thousand flocked to this theatre, and people who reported not generally liking Shakespeare plays said that the productions they saw in this theatre changed their minds.[31] If nothing else, the presence of the actors in the same volume of space as the audience, with no proscenium-arch frame, no front curtain, and no difference in light between the stage and the house, was a compelling experience.

The extensive repertory to be done in this theatre was far more controversial than any failings of the architecture. In order to adapt to the need of a busy audience, and in order to generate the necessary income from a small house, there had to be a great many performances, and they had to be short. In 1912 the producers at the Earls Court Globe opted for simply doing scenes from Shakespeare. Stevens thought this ineffective since it left the audience with no context in which to put what they were seeing. Payne, in one of his most serious divergences from Poel, had always argued that the plays could be cut intertextually as long as the meter was preserved and the "melodic line" of the action was maintained.[32] So Stevens, with the assistance of B. Iden Payne and Theodore Viehman, undertook the task of putting this idea to the ultimate test. Plays that generally took from one hour, forty-five minutes to two hours, fifteen minutes to perform using Poel's methods of rapid delivery were to be cut down to thirty-five to forty-five minutes.[33] The texts, many of which remain available even today, are quite remarkable but hardly to be recommended to lovers of Shakespeare. The shorter plays were selected to start the season, *The Taming of the Shrew* and *The Comedy of Errors* (arranged by B. Iden Payne), *A Midsummer Night's Dream* (arranged by Theodore Viehman), *Julius Caesar*, and *Macbeth* (by Thomas Wood Stevens) among others. But even with the short plays it was clear that no amount of intertextual cutting was going to get them down to forty-five minutes. So the plays had to be refocused. In *Shrew*, for example, the induction was cut and the play ended with act 4, scene 4, just before Kate's conversion to dutiful wife. *Julius Caesar* was focused on Caesar, with most commentary on Brutus removed. That script ended with Mark Anthony's final speech in act 3. The plan for *A Midsummer Night's Dream* was to edit it into two shows, one of the mechanicals and one of the lovers. But the mechanicals show was done first, and it proved so popular that the lovers edition was never done. As the acting company got better, more text was added back into most of the plays and the eventual running times were extended to fifty-five minutes. When the longer plays like *Hamlet* and *King Lear* were added to the repertory, they ran between one hour, thirty minutes and two hours. The Globe company, however, was doing a repertory of seven performances a day, with eight performances on Saturday and Sunday, so the longer plays had to be put last on the bill.

William Poel died in 1934, but it is probably not fair to say that these heavily edited texts were the death of him. They were excellent thumbnail sketches of the plays, which were, by all accounts, very well received by the public and, more remarkably, by the critics. After rehearsing the plays for his part of the Chicago repertory in 1934, B. Iden Payne left to become artistic director at the Shakespeare Memorial Theatre in Stratford-on-Avon, a position he held until 1942. In doing this he took the staging techniques he had developed with Stevens in the United States back to England to influence a new generation of directors there. Payne was hired to replace W. Bridges-Adams, another important director who had been heavily influenced by Poel's ideas as taught by Nugent Monck and one of the original actors in the 1912 Globe at Earls Court.

The Globe company performed their grueling repertory at the Chicago Globe from the end of May to October 1934. The company moved to San Diego for the 1935 California Pacific International Exhibition, where a slightly larger Globe, based on the Chicago model but seating 560, was designed for them by architect George Vernan Russell. This time, at least, there was no roof over the yard. The Globe company was invited back for the 1936 season, but they were already scheduled to transfer to the Texas Centennial Exposition in Dallas, where a third Globe, again based on the Chicago model, had been designed for them by architect Hans Oberhammer. The solution to this problem was to create a replacement company, the Fortune Company, for the second San Diego season. A third company, the Blackfriars company, also had to be created for the 1936 season because yet another Globe, this one designed by architect James William Thomas, had been built for them at the Great Lakes Exposition in Cleveland, Ohio. Among the members of the Blackfriars company in Cleveland was Sam Wanamaker, a native of Chicago who had gotten the theatre bug from seeing the Chicago Globe in the summer of 1934. It was the inspiration of this experience that prompted him to dedicate the last twenty-three years of his life, from 1970 to 1993, to the building of the Globe theatre in London, a project that was finally realized in 1997, three and a half years after his death and exactly one hundred years after such a project had first been called for by William Poel. This is a fitting connection because just as Stevens's Globe marked an explosion of Elizabethan Revival activities in the 1930s, Wanamaker's Globe has generated an equivalent explosion today. The history of theatre in the twentieth century would not have been the same without Poel's tenacious dedication to the study of Shakespeare's stagecraft; the history of theatre in the twenty-first century is bound to be equally impacted by Wanamaker's tenacious determination to see Poel's dream fulfilled, and that determination started at the Chicago Globe in 1934.

Over a three-year period, from 1934 to 1937, at the height of the Great Depression, Thomas Wood Stevens and his three acting companies produced eighteen plays by Shakespeare, plus *Doctor Faustus*, in five thousand performances seen by more than two million people either at the Globe reconstructions built in Chicago, San Diego, Dallas, and Cleveland or on tours, several of which were sponsored by the Federal Theatre Project.[34] (A fifth Globe was built for the World's Fair in 1939 in New York, but this was under the direction of Margaret Webster, who went on to become one of America's premier directors after World War II.) There was no pretence of following Poel's first axiom of original staging practices (as it was described by Casson above), using "the full text in its proper order without interpolations or rearrangement."[35] But Poel's other ideas, including the use of Elizabethan costuming, were employed. Among the first people hired to work for the Globe company, in fact, was Lucy Barton, who later became one of the most influential costume-design educators in America. She had learned her craft at Carnegie Tech under Harold Geoghegan and had perfected her knowledge of Elizabethan costume through working with the wardrobe from Poel's Elizabethan Stage Society, parts of which Stevens had arranged for Carnegie Tech to purchase. Years later she noted that they used Elizabethan costumes because they were the most appropriate to the action, were historically correct, were visually interesting, and were especially practical for an extensive repertory.[36] Stevens was certainly aware of the argument that since the Elizabethans acted in what was for them a heightened modern dress, we ought to do the same. But as an art historian he was aware that there is such a thing as period style. We generally accept in everyday life that there is a relationship between the way we speak and the clothing we wear. It is hard to imagine anyone doing *West Side Story* in the clothing of the mid-1970s disco era, for example. But the lesson somehow eludes even the most competent costume designers when it comes to selecting an appropriate style to match Shakespearean language. Shakespearean costuming need not be Elizabethan, but it does need an elegance of style that complements the ornateness of the poetic language.

In 1935, while Stevens's Globe company was moving to San Diego, where they opened their new theatre on May 29, Angus L. Bowmer was taking the first steps to founding the Oregon Shakespeare Festival in Ashland, which would open just five weeks later. Bowmer had met B. Iden Payne in 1930, when Payne worked as a guest director at the University of Washington between stepping down as chair at Carnegie Tech and joining Stevens at the Goodman. For the productions of *Cymbeline* and *Love's Labour's Lost* that Payne did in Washington, he used the kind of stage he had been using to explore original staging practices at Carnegie Tech for some years, one that contained all the basic elements of Poel's Fortune fit-up.[37] John Conway, acting chair of the Department of Theatre at Washington and a recent graduate of the Carnegie Tech program, was very familiar with Payne's work and designed the Elizabethan stage used for these 1930 productions. As a student at the university, Bowmer not only acted in these productions, but he also helped build the stage. So when he instituted what he so boldly called the "First Annual Shakespeare Festival" in Ashland, he simply duplicated what he remembered of the Conway set. Bowmer also applied Payne's modified Elizabethan staging techniques as he understood them, focusing on the "storytelling rhythm" of the plays. Whereas Payne, against his better judgment, had always included intermissions in his productions of Shakespeare, Bowmer did without them.[38] After six seasons the festival closed for the duration of World War II. During the war, in 1942, John Cranford Adams published the *Globe Playhouse*, based on his 1934 dissertation "The Structure of the Globe Playhouse and Stage." J. C. Adams's ideas on the Globe quickly came to dominate all thinking on the topic. So when the Oregon festival reopened in 1947, a much more elaborate stage, designed by Richard L. Hay and based on the J. C. Adams reconstruction, was erected. The current even more elaborate stage at the festival was built in 1959 (also designed by Hay) and the present configuration of the house, the Allen Pavilion, was added in 1992. To this day the festival features the sign "America's First Elizabethan Theatre," but its 1935 manifestation was not as Elizabethan as the Harvard stage of 1895 and was well behind the Folger (1932) and the Globes at Chicago (1934) and San Diego (1935).

Meanwhile the San Diego venture followed a similar path. When the International Exhibition closed, the community raised money to save the "Old Globe," rebuilding it in more permanent materials than had been used for the temporary exhibition. In the process of this rebuilding it got slightly smaller and acquired a roof over the yard. The San Diego Community Theater used this Globe until it was turned over to the Navy in 1941. The San Diego Old Globe theatre was reopened by Craig Noel in 1947, and B. Iden Payne was brought in to direct *Twelfth Night* there for the 1949 season. It did not become the home of the San Diego National Shakespeare Festival, however, until 1954. The San Diego Old Globe was destroyed in a fire in 1978. The current, more-modern building opened in 1981.

In his autobiography Bowmer described a prewar visit to London in which he was told of a "New Globe Theatre" reconstruction to be built near the Globe's original site on Bankside. The project was to include a library, museum, and pub. An acting company, he was told, had already been selected and was performing in a place called "The Ring."[39]

This was undoubtedly the Globe-Mermaid Association of England and America's 1935 proposal to build a Globe reconstruction where the Tate Modern Gallery stands today, just a few yards west of Wanamaker's Globe.[40] The outbreak of war put a stop to this project. After the war, in 1951, an Elizabethan theatre reconstruction called the Mermaid Theatre (showcasing the work of C. Walter Hodges and Joseph Bertram among others) was built on the opposite side of the river, but it was not on anything like the scale of the 1935 proposal.[41]

In the United States the most significant Elizabethan stage of the 1950s was the Hofstra University Shakespeare Festival Globe Stage in Hempstead, New York. This was a ⅝-scale version of the famous Globe reconstruction by J. C. Adams, the university's president from 1944 to 1964. It was a Globe fit-up designed by Donald H. Swinney that was put up in the Calkins Gymnasium each season from 1951 to 1957 and then transferred to the Hofstra Playhouse, now the Adams Playhouse, where it continues to be used. Like Poel's Fortune fit-up the Adams Globe fit-up is designed to explore the theories of one man. Numerous other institutions have experimented with Elizabethan stage sets, including Yale (1938–41), University of Illinois (1941), and even Columbus College in Columbus, Georgia (1970), but none have been more influential than this Hofstra stage.[42]

By far the most significant theatre to be built during the 1950s, however, was the Stratford Festival Theatre in Ontario, Canada. This theatre began its life in 1953 as a tent theatre featuring a modern Elizabethan-style stage designed by Tanya Moiseiwitsch to the specifications of the Poel-inspired English director Tyrone Guthrie. The stage was far more like the open stage Jacques Copeau had built at the Théâtre du Vieux Colombier in Paris in 1913 than it was to any of the reconstructed stages I have reviewed here. It was a frank admission of what nearly all the directors in the Elizabethan Revival had argued at some point in their careers: that it was not possible to build an authentic Elizabethan stage and that such a stage was not necessary in order to learn what could be learned about Elizabethan staging practices. What was needed, they argued, was a stage that maintained the essential spatial characteristics of an Elizabethan stage, and that is what Moiseiwitsch and Guthrie claimed for the Stratford, Ontario, stage. Oddly, this logic was not carried out into the house. There it was thought to be perfectly acceptable to employ Greek-style seating for 2,258. Nothing essential of the spatial characteristics of Elizabethan seating arrangements was being preserved by this arrangement. But regardless, in 1957 this arrangement was made permanent. In 1997 the space underwent a substantial renovation during which the seating remained Greek, but the capacity was reduced to

1,824. This theatre inspired the later very successful open stages at the Chichester Festival in England (1962) and the Guthrie Theatre in Minneapolis (1963).

The 1960s saw the creation of the Utah Shakespeare Festival (1962), whose director, Fred C. Adams, consciously attempted to duplicate the Oregon Shakespeare Festival experience. As in Oregon, Utah started with a simple Elizabethan stage, changed to a more substantial stage (1971), and finally added a permanent polygonal gallery (1977), at which time the theatre was renamed the Adams Theatre. In 1965 schoolteacher Marjorie Morris fulfilled her lifelong dream of creating a Globe reconstruction when, after years of constant fund-raising, she managed to open the Globe of the Great Southwest in Odessa, Texas. The 1970s saw the start of Wanamaker's plans to build a Globe theatre project in London much like the Globe-Mermaid Association of England and America had planned in 1935. The complex international organization he created to move this project forward and his use of scholarly meetings to develop the details of the project had an extraordinary impact on the Elizabethan Revival for the remainder of that century as project after project pushed forward either in emulation of the London Globe or in an attempt to get ahead of it. Wanamaker called his project the third Globe, but by 1979 that name was appropriated by the Detroit Globe project, spearheaded by Leonard Leone of Wayne State University. In the meantime R. Thad Taylor announced his intentions to build a Globe in the Santa Monica mountains and Seashore National Urban Park for the Shakespeare Society of America, which operated out of what they called a half-size Globe in Los Angeles. All three projects stalled, and the only reconstruction attempt to move forward was that of George Murcell and his St. George's Elizabethan Theatre Trust. The trust was started in 1969 to build an Elizabethan stage designed by C. Walter Hodges inside a circular, mid-nineteenth-century church in Tufnell Park, north London. The theatre finally opened in 1976, but it had little success, and the galleries that were to be a key component of the structure were never built.[43] The most important Elizabethan-style theatres in the 1980s, like those of the 1920s, were once again in England and Japan, the Swan Theatre in Stratford-upon-Avon (1986), and the Tokyo Globe (1988). The Swan was designed by English architect Michael Reardon and was fully funded by American philanthropist Fred Koch. America got something back from this project, however, when the new Chicago Shakespeare Theatre at Navy Pier (1999) was modeled after it.[44] Indeed the 1990s saw an explosion of Globe reconstructions after the opening of Wanamaker's Shakespeare Globe Theatre in 1997 (see Schormann, this volume). I will only note here that among the many projects it has inspired, including the second Globe for Shenandoah Shakespeare and the Rose for Shakespeare and Company noted earlier, reconstructions have been planned for the Mall of America in Minneapolis, for Black Mountain in Las Vegas, and for Governor's Island in New York City.

These attempts to reconstruct Elizabethan spaces have reminded us, when we needed such reminders, that theatre is about more than text; it is also about actors and buildings and costumes and music and movement styles and a myriad of other details that make up its complete system of signs. And it has taught us that when we are dissatisfied with the status quo, we are not limited to our own resources to begin new approaches; we can look back at what others have learned about how theatre can work and benefit from their experience even though we are not the same people as they were. The more detailed and thorough our examinations of the past are, the more of its complexity we can see and the more sophisticated the solutions our examinations can inspire. The attempts at recapturing the original staging practices of Shakespeare's day encourage that kind of concern for detail and thoroughness. I cannot agree with those critics who say that it is somehow harmful, misguided, or irrelevant.

Dennis Kennedy has pointed out that theatrical productions are "manufactured for a highly specific geographical and sociopolitical audience" and that over time "they will lose their significant connection to the culture they invoke" and therefore must be reinterpreted.[45] Such observations are often used to underscore the futility of projects like Elizabethan theatre reconstruction. We cannot be Elizabethans, so how can we appreciate Elizabethan staging practices? But what are the parameters of those reinterpretations Kennedy says we must do? If the past has no relevance to the present, we should be writing new plays, not reinterpreting old ones. But if there is something in these old plays that is worth conveying to those living in the present, we must translate that something into terms a contemporary audience will understand. And surely we want the translators to be competent in both the contemporary language and the language of the source. The reconstruction of Elizabethan spaces and their use for the exploration of original staging practices make us better translators. It is not possible to have been a regular theatregoer without having seen a lot of experimental work. We have all seen weird and wonderful productions of Elizabethan plays, we have all seen weird and tedious productions of Elizabethan plays, and I'm sorry to say we have all seen weird and just plain silly productions of Elizabethan plays. These hit-and-miss efforts, I submit, are the result of incompetent translation either by those who know their own theatrical language but cannot read the source language in the Elizabethan texts or by those who know the source but have little command of the modern language of the stage. The attempt at recapturing original staging practices, however, forces one to learn the source language in a systematic and disciplined way—and in minute detail. It requires that we recognize that learning a language is not just a matter of knowing the words; it is also a matter of learning the grammar, the syntax, and, in theatre, the ways in which space gives meaning to text. It may never be possible for us to become fluent, and who could tell us if we were, but this does not mean we cannot develop a good working knowledge of the theatrical language of Shakespeare's day.

To conclude, I do not know what our attempts at recreating Elizabethan playing spaces have taught us about Elizabethan plays. I do believe, however, that this work has given us invaluable insights into theatre in general and that the lessons we have learned from the various attempts have the potential to expand the way we think about theatre in our own day. Historically, the quest for original staging practices has preserved essential parts of our cultural history and allowed theatre artists to influence the present by taking a careful look at the past. The quest to understand Elizabethan staging practices has helped us to tell compelling stories by moving their action always forward, has revealed the value of putting the actors and audience in the same volume of space, has offered new insights into what I have identified as the difference between audience participation and the authorization for audiences to respond, and has made us rethink the nature of audience comfort in a theatre space. (No one believed, when we were promoting the London Globe project, for example, that five hundred to seven hundred people would pay to stand at every performance, but they do.) The new generation of recreated Elizabethan spaces will allow us to explore the relationship between language and costume and music in ways that have never been done before. And the search for original staging practices can instill a discipline that could well lead to an entirely new approach to theatre in our "anything passes for art" culture. This, so far, is my answer to the question that started me on this exploration, why Elizabethan spaces?

Notes

1. For some examples of these arguments see Andrew Gurr, "Maximal and Minimal Texts: Shakespeare V. the Globe," *Shakespeare Survey* 52 (1999): 77; and Kathleen O. Irace, *Reforming the "Bad" Quartos: Performance and Provenance of Six Shakespearean First Editions* (Newark: University of Delaware Press, 1994).

2. See Jonathan Bates and Russell Jackson, eds., *Shakespeare: An Illustrated Stage History* (Oxford: Oxford University Press, 1996), 43, 50.

3. See Jill L. Levenson, "The Recovery of the Elizabethan Stage," *Elizabethan Theatre* 9 (1986): 208–9.

4. William Poel, *Shakespeare in the Theatre* (London: Sidgwick and Jackson, 1913), 33–38.

5. Bates and Jackson, *Shakespeare*, 64.

6. Robert Speaight, *William Poel and the Elizabethan Revival* (Cambridge, MA: Harvard University Press, 1954), 50–57.

7. Theatre professionals throughout Europe were interested in this process of recapturing pre-proscenium production methods. These professionals included not only Poel in England and Savits in Germany but also Nikolia Evreinov in Russia, W. B. Yeats in Ireland, and both André Antoine and Aurélien Lugné-Poë in France, just to name a few of the more prominent practitioners. Much of the work of the revivalists is covered in Dennis Kennedy, *Looking at Shakespeare* (Cambridge, UK: Cambridge University Press, 1993), 25–42; but for the attempt by Yeats to bring medieval drama to the Abbey Theatre see my *Shakespeare at the Maddermarket: Nugent Monck and the Norwich Players* (Ann Arbor: UMI Research, 1986), 18–24; for Evreinov and the Ancient Theatre in St. Petersburg see Spencer Golub, *Evreinov: The Theatre of Paradox and Transformation* (Ann Arbor: UMI Research, 1984), 107–43; and for Antoine's work with French drama see Oscar Gross Brockett and Robert R. Findlay, *Century of Innovation,* 2nd ed. (Englewood Cliffs, NJ: Prentice-Hall, 1991), 111.

8. Levenson, "Recovery of the Elizabethan Stage," 215–16.

9. I have argued elsewhere that this 27½-foot stage depth may be incorrect. See my "Reconstructing Shakespeare's Theatre," in *New Issues in the Reconstruction of Shakespeare's Theatre,* ed. Franklin J. Hildy (New York: Peter Lang, 1990), 6.

10. See Marion O'Connor, "'Useful in the Year 1999': William Poel and Shakespeare's 'Build of Stage,'" in *Shakespeare Survey* 52 (1999): 17–32, for a full and somewhat negative account of Poel's use of the Fortune fit-up.

11. See Levenson, "Recovery of the Elizabethan Stage," 221–23.

12. Quoted in Marvin Carlson, *Theories of the Theatre,* expanded ed. (Ithaca, NY: Cornell University Press, 1993), 288.

13. Quoted in *Daily Chronicle,* Sep. 13, 1913.

14. George Pierce Baker makes similar arguments in *The Development of Shakespeare as a Dramatist* (London: Macmillan, 1920), 7.

15. See Sir Lewis Casson, "William Poel and the Modern Theatre," *Listener,* Jan. 10, 1952, 56.

16. Ben Iden Payne, *A Life in a Wooden O* (New Haven, CT: Yale University Press, 1977), 87.

17. Ibid., 88.

18. Tyrone Guthrie, *In Various Directions* (London: McGraw-Hill, 1965), 64.

19. See Martin White, "William Poel's Globe," *Theatre Notebook* 53, no. 3 (1999): 146–62.

20. See Franklin J. Hildy, "Reconstructing Shakespeare's Theatre," in *New*

Issues in the Reconstruction of Shakespeare's Theatre, ed. Franklin J. Hildy (New York: Peter Lang, 1990), 1–37, esp. 18.

21. The most complete report on the Globe of 1912 is Marion F. O'Connor's "Theatre of the Empire: 'Shakespeare's England at Earls Court,' 1912," in *Shakespeare Reproduced: The Text in History and Ideology*, ed. Jean E. Howard and Marion F. O'Connor (New York: Methuen, 1987), 68–98. See also Ralph G. Martin, *Jennie: The Life of Lady Randolph Churchill*, vol. 2, *The Dramatic Years, 1885–1921* (New York: Signet, 1970), 316. For Poel's negative reaction to the Earls Court Globe see William Poel, *Shakespeare in the Theatre* (London: Sidgwick and Jackson, 1913), 208–12.

22. For a description of the Carnegie Institute of Technology program see Thomas Wood Stevens, "A School of the Theatre Arts," *Drama* 16 (Nov. 1914): 635–39. For the earliest report on Poel's visit there see Stephen Allard, "William Poel in America," *Theatre Arts* (Nov. 1916): 24–26.

23. Payne, *Wooden O*, 90.

24. Ben Iden Payne outlines his own approach to "modified Elizabethan staging" in *Wooden O* (162–72).

25. The 1904 Harvard stage and what was learned from it are outlined in Geo[rge] P. Baker, "Theaterschau: 'Hamlet' on an Elizabethan Stage," *Jahrbuch der Deutschen Shakespeare-Gesellschaft* 41 (1905): 296–301.

26. Herbert Berry, "Americans in the Playhouse," *Shakespeare Studies* 9 (1976): 31–44. For a history of American involvement in theoretical reconstructions of Elizabethan playhouses see James Stinson, "Reconstructions of Elizabethan Public Playhouses," in *Studies in the Elizabethan Theatre*, ed. Charles T. Prouty (Hamden, CT: Shoestring, 1961).

27. Baker, *Development of Shakespeare*, 87.

28. See my *Shakespeare at the Maddermarket*, 109–30.

29. The architect of the Folger, Paul Philippe Cret, does not mention the Maddermarket in his description of the Folger theatre. See Paul Philippe Cret, "The Building," in *The Folger Shakespeare Library, Washington* (Washington, DC: Trustees of Amherst College, 1933), 31–36 [the theatre is discussed on 34–35]. But the sources he does mention would not have shown this double arrangement of doors; and his academic adviser, John Quincy Adams, does not show such doors in his own theoretical reconstruction in *A Life of Shakespeare* (Boston: Houghton Mifflin, 1923), 286. Photos of the Maddermarket, on the other hand, were generally available, and Monck's work there was especially well known after he staged *Everyman* at the Canterbury Festival in 1929.

30. Hildy, "Reconstructing Shakespeare's Theatre," 27, 63–64.

31. See Donna Rose Feldman, *An Historical Study of Thomas Wood Stevens' Globe Theatre Company, 1934–1937* (PhD diss., University of Iowa, 1953). Additional information on the Chicago Globe can be found in Rosemary Kegl, "'[W]rapping Togas over Elizabethan Garb': Tabloid Shakespeare at the 1934 Chicago World's Fair," *Renaissance Drama*, n.s., 28 (1997): 73–97.

32. Payne, *Wooden O*, 190.

33. Over three years the Globe companies performed edited versions of *The Taming of the Shrew*, *The Comedy of Errors* (arranged by B. Iden Payne), *A*

Midsummer Night's Dream (arranged by Theodore Viehman), *Julius Caesar, All's Well That Ends Well, As You Like It* (B. Iden Payne), *Doctor Faustus, Macbeth, King Lear, Twelfth Night, Much Ado about Nothing, Hamlet, Winter's Tale, The Merry Wives of Windsor, Henry VIII, The Tempest, The Two Gentlemen of Verona, The Life and Death of Falstaff* (sounds like *Chimes at Midnight*), and *Romeo and Juliet*.

34. Melvin R. White, "Thomas Wood Stevens: Creative Pioneer," *Educational Theatre Journal* 3, no. 4 (Dec. 1951): 290. Note: the article says nineteen plays, but one was *Doctor Faustus*.

35. Casson, "William Poel," 56.

36. Lucy Barton, "Why Not Costume Shakespeare according to Shakespeare?" *Educational Theatre Journal* 19 (Apr. 1967): 549–55.

37. Angus L. Bowmer has outlined Payne's influence on him in *As I Remember Adam* (Ashland: Oregon Shakespearean Festival Association, 1975), 25–32. For his report on how he copied the set Payne had used for his first productions at Ashland see 76 and 79.

38. Edward Brubaker and Mary Brubaker, *Golden Fire* (Ashland: Oregon Shakespearean Festival Association, 1985), 44. Bowmer outlined his approach to original practices in his *Chapbook #2: Shreds and Patches: Acting and Directing on the Ashland Elizabethan Stage* (Ashland: Oregon Shakespearean Festival Association, 1979).

39. Bowmer, *As I Remember Adam*, 106.

40. Andrew Gurr with John Orrell, *Rebuilding Shakespeare's Globe* (New York: Routledge, 1989), 32–34.

41. Gerard Fay, ed., *Mermaid* (London: Mermaid Theatre, 1953).

42. For the Hofstra and Columbus College stages see Glen Loney and Patricia MacKay, *The Shakespeare Complex* (New York: Drama Book Specialists, 1975), 174–82; for the Yale and University of Illinois stages see Cecile de Banke, *Shakespearean Stage Production: Then and Now* (London: Hutchinson, 1954), photo insert between 64–65.

43. See C. Walter Hodges, S. Schoenbaum, and Leonard Leone, eds., *The Third Globe* (Detroit, MI: Wayne State University Press, 1981); Loney and MacKay, *The Shakespeare Complex*, 86–87; and *Shakespeare at St. Georges* (London: St. Georges Theatre, 1979).

44. See Ronnie Mulryne and Margaret Shewring, *This Golden Round* (Stratford-on-Avon: Mulryne and Shewring, 1989); and Minoru Fujita and Arata Isozaki, *The Globe* (Tokyo: Shinjuku-Nishitoyama, 1988).

45. Dennis Kennedy, *Looking at Shakespeare* (Cambridge, UK: Cambridge University Press, 1993), 4.

Shakespeare's Globe Theatre

Where History Meets Innovation

Vanessa Schormann

"ALL THE WORLD'S A STAGE," says Jacques in Shakespeare's *As You Like It*. When Queen Elizabeth II opened the reconstructed Globe Theatre on Bankside in London on June 12, 1997, all the world was looking at the new theatre—and its architects, builders, directors, and actors were eager to know whether the world liked it. Since then, audiences, scholars, critics, and tourists from all over the world have had the opportunity to visit and view the Globe, to enjoy performances, criticize or praise them, and discuss opinions about a theatre building that had not been in existence for nearly four hundred years.

The Globe is a phenomenon that is discussed controversially, not only among scholars. The German critic Ekkehart Krippendorf, for example, says, "The reconstruction of the Globe Theatre, Shakespeare's playhouse, is from the point of theatre history the event of the century. To express it directly and enthusiastically: here and now a new epoch begins."[1] Other critics, like John Drakakis, define the Globe as a model of a theatre that has "long outlived its social and cultural relevance." For Drakakis the Globe is not a reconstruction but the fourth Globe, "erected upon nostalgia and sentiment."[2]

Today, the Globe is one of the most successful theatres in London, playing to over 90 percent capacity each year. And, being listed in every London city guide, it has become one of the most popular tourist sites. One reason for the Globe's attraction is the fact that it is connected with William Shakespeare, a dramatist whose plays are performed in nearly every country around the world. After visiting Shakespeare's birthplace in Stratford-upon-Avon tourists come to visit his workplace in London.

Being a reconstruction of a historical building, the Globe attracts with its historical look. Built with handcraft and authentic materials, the building is a fascinating piece of art and therefore not only serves the arts that are presented in it but also deserves to be admired for itself. Today, the Globe in London is a building that is a museum and a theatre, as well as an object of research, and therefore has something to offer for everyone: tourists, theatre audiences, and scholars.

The Globe in London is not the only replica of Shakespeare's theatre. Even before the American actor Sam Wanamaker started his campaign to rebuild Shakespeare's theatre, there had been various attempts to rebuild the Globe. In fact, in the last hundred years more replicas of the Elizabethan theatre and its stage were built around the world than there had been amphitheatres in Shakespeare's time. Today, apart from London, we can watch the Bard's plays in copies of the Globe in the United States of America, in Japan, in the Czech Republic, in Germany, and in Lappland.

Although the Elizabethan playhouses only existed for about seventy years—no purpose-built open-air playhouse structure existed in England before 1567, none was built after 1623, and all were closed down in 1642—there is no other stage form that has influenced the history of theatre more than that of the Shakespearean theatres. It's a phenomenon that has not lost its fascination over four centuries and especially since nineteenth-century scholars all over the world published numerous theories in which they analyzed the stage form, stage conventions, and playgoing of that time.

What were the reasons for trying to rebuild Shakespeare's Globe, and what are the discoveries we can make, now that there are so many Globes in the world? Can a historical reconstruction be an innovative theatre?

Here I will try to answer these questions by drawing attention to the various attempts at rebuilding Shakespeare's Globe. I will demonstrate how the replicas are linked to the reconstruction in London and comment on the controversial debate that accompanies the Globe today. Finally, I would like to introduce some of the discoveries that have been made in London so far, especially concerning the audience. While trying to follow that path from past to present and into the future, we have to concentrate on three inseparable elements that are connected with the Globe: architecture, play, and audience.

Any Globe replica today is an invention based on the research material of the last four hundred years. Shakespeare's Globe—the theatre Shakespeare acted in and wrote most of his plays for—was not an original building; it was itself a replica of a playhouse called "The Theatre," which James Burbage had built in 1576. After the Theatre's lease of ground had run out, the actors dismantled it and carried the timbers over the River Thames, where they rebuilt it outside the city walls, naming it "The Globe." It was opened in 1599 and became one of the most successful theatres of the time. After the closure of all London playhouses in 1642, most of them were destroyed either by men or time, and this special type of theatre building disappeared. The chance for a further development of the Elizabethan playhouses was missed. If there had not been an "Elizabethan Revival" in the nineteenth century, supported by discoveries of historic material, the form and function of the Elizabethan theatre would have been forgotten.

The playhouses in Shakespeare's time were new inventions based on old traditions; the booth stage, courtyard inn, and royal masque had a formative influence on the development of the playhouse's form. The plays written for the theatres combined traditions of the past with newly invented conventions. Examining Shakespeare's dramaturgy, we realize that it is greatly influenced by the specific elements of the Elizabethan stage. The pillars, doors, and balcony played an important part, as did the audience that surrounded the stage on three sides.

In 1599 visiting the Globe was an event for all ages and people from different social statuses. Among the audience were also visitors from abroad, and it is mainly owing to their accounts in diaries and travel journals that we know something about the theatre and its use in Shakespeare's time. Among the most important documents is de Witt's drawing of the Swan, as well as the contracts of the Fortune and Hope Theatres. The Fortune contract, for example, tells the Globe builder Peter Street to build the Fortune just like the Globe. Therefore, the Fortune, built in 1600, could be called the first replica of the Globe. Bearing in mind that the Fortune was a square building, one could argue that architectural modifications and improvements were already done a year after the Globe's opening, which might justify all the modifications that were attempted on the various replicas since.

After the closure of the playhouses in the seventeenth century, Shakespeare's theatre and its specific elements—the thrust stage, the pillars and roof, the balcony, the galleries, the pit, and the tiring house, as well as the stage conventions of that time—had become old-fashioned. With the loss of these features the dramaturgy of Shakespeare's plays had to be changed and adapted to the environment where they were presented.

The result was that his plays were no longer performed in their original version, and most of the plays of Shakespeare's contemporaries disappeared completely. It was only in the nineteenth century that Shakespeare's plays were rediscovered as fascinating pieces of poetry. The desire to present the plays in their original form led to a new interest in the stage and theatre for which the plays were written.

The first who took the challenge of rebuilding the stage was the German dramaturge Ludwig Tieck. He realized that for producing Shakespeare's text with the original dramaturgy one needed an empty stage. His aim, therefore, was to invent a new stage where plays could be acted without any change of theatrical decoration and where the audience had to concentrate on the text, which does give all the necessary pieces of information. Tieck based his model of the ideal Shakespeare stage on the discovered Fortune contract and asked Gottfried Semper, the architect of the Semper Opera in Dresden, to draw a plan of the Fortune.

The plan was then reproduced as a stage set for Tieck's famous production of *A Midsummer Night's Dream* in the Potsdamer Schloß-theater in 1843. The set consisted of a shallow stage with pillars and a tiring house in the background. Although the reconstruction of the Fortune was only in the form of a stage set, it was the first attempt to place the action onstage closer to the audience and to stir their imagination by omitting an expressive stage decoration.

Inspired by Tieck's approach and aiming to reform the nineteenth-century stage, artistic director Karl von Perfall, director Jocza Savits, and stage technician Carl Lautenschlaeger built the "Muenchner Shakespeare Buehne" in 1889 in Germany. They were not interested in reconstructing an old stage form but wanted to create an ideal stage for the presentation of Shakespeare's plays. They based their approach on the writings of theatre historian Rudolph Genée, who argued that Shakespeare's Globe was the perfection of all theatres and consisted of a bare stage with decoration panels in the background. The Munich Shakespeare Stage had a stage that thrust into the auditorium, where most of the action took place, while in the background various prospectuses were used for scene changes.

More or less at the same time in England the "Elizabethan Revival" was led by actor and director William Poel, who had been inspired by the Munich stage. With his "Fortune fit-up," as well as with his ideas, plans, and model for rebuilding the Globe, he inspired the architect Edward Lutyens, who built the first full-scale replica of the Globe at Earl's Court in London in 1912. In the United States Thomas Wood Stevens and Ben Iden Payne followed with their approaches of rebuilding the Globe in Chicago, Dallas, Cleveland, San Diego, and New York in the mid-1930s.[3]

The early Globes in England and the United States demonstrate that although the original attempt was to find a stage or theatre that helped to produce Shakespeare's dramaturgy in a more adequate way, the buildings that were developed were mainly fulfilling the purpose of being a tourist attraction. Interestingly enough, the success of the Globe as a tourist attraction led to the idea of organizing annual Shakespeare festivals in North America.

Today, nearly every US state has its own festival. Not all of them present Shakespeare on reconstructed Elizabethan stages, but a few have built a replica of the Globe. The most famous North American festivals that offer Shakespeare on reconstructed Elizabethan stages are the Oregon Shakespeare Festival, founded by Angus L. Bowmer in 1935 in Ashland, Oregon; the Utah Shakespearean Festival in Cedar City, Utah, founded by Fred C. Adams in 1962; and the Stratford Festival in Stratford, Ontario, in Canada, founded by Tom Patterson in 1953. Instead of rebuilding the three-story galleries, the theatres in Ashland and Stratford use a Greek-style auditorium. The audience still surrounds the stage on three sides, but the intimacy of the Globe interior, as well as the closeness to the action onstage, is lost.

In Odessa, Texas, a young teacher attempted to rebuild the Globe. Like in Ashland, the architect based his plans on John Cranford Adams's Globe model from 1942. Looking at the result today, it seems more than ironic that in 1968, when "The Globe of the Great Southwest" was opened, the scholar Allardyce Nicoll called it "the most nearly authentic replica of Shakespeare's own Globe anywhere on earth."[4] In the 1970s they were running a successful annual Shakespeare Festival, but today the Globe in Odessa is used only by amateurs who perform Shakespeare with great enthusiasm in front of small audiences.

And there are more links in the chain. In 1934 the fifteen-year-old Sam Wanamaker had gone to see the Globe at the World's Fair in Chicago. Two years later he had joined Thomas Wood Stevens's company as a young actor, playing minor characters in the Cleveland Globe. In the 1940s, when Wanamaker went to London, expecting to be able to see the original Globe there, all he could find was a memorial sign at the fence of a brewery saying: "Here stood Shakespeare's Globe in 1599." In 1970 Wanamaker went to the Greater London Council and made the same proposal William Poel had made one hundred years before: he asked them to rebuild Shakespeare's Globe on Bankside.

Wanamaker's intention was to build a Shakespeare theatre and an International Shakespeare Center in order to educate and entertain the audience with Shakespeare's plays. Remembering the intimate atmosphere of the "wooden O" from his time in Cleveland, he wanted to build a Globe where audiences and actors share one room and a unique experience. The international campaign he started in order to raise money for this courageous project was accompanied by the myth that

Shakespeare's Globe would become a Disney-like Globe built by an American Hollywood actor.

What most of the critics do not know is that in the beginning Wanamaker had no special interest in rebuilding the Globe in an authentic way. It was the academics who suggested that it be rebuilt as an authentic reconstruction. Wanamaker took the challenge, and the scholars started with all the research that brought to daylight what we know today about the theatre in Shakespeare's time.

There is no doubt that without Wanamaker's Globe project a lot of the knowledge that we have today about the Elizabethan theatre might not have been discovered. Only the task to rebuild the Globe as original as possible revealed details about its size, form, and function. The discoveries of the Rose's foundations in 1988–89 and those of the Globe in 1989 were also great revelations.

Although the scholars were unable to rescue the archaeological foundations, the excavations gave some valuable information on the Globe's size and dimensions. Nevertheless, we have to admit our knowledge about the Globe is still quite poor. All the sources, the ones found since the nineteenth century, as well as the research results that were based on them, are not enough to rebuild any of the Elizabethan theatres authentically. The question of authenticity concerning the building or the acting onstage has been the subject of many discussions among scholars.

While in the field of music it has become a common habit to play historical music on originally reconstructed instruments, the search for the lost theatrical past of the Globe is critically debated, and we have to ask, What exactly is authenticity? C. Walter Hodges defines it as follows:

> Authenticity . . . is the proper end of scholarship, in the case of actually building the Globe, the scholar is faced with both a quaking dilemma and an awful responsibility. . . . Whatever is done, the result is going to be judged as *a work of art*. The scholarship, the scientific study that has gone into it all and may claim to be its validation, will in the end have been completely absorbed into the fabric, and what now stands upon the ground *is* a work of art.[5]

Theatre historian Franklin J. Hildy says: "Authenticity has always been—and will always be—compromised by our lack of knowledge,"[6] and he is right. Nobody can say with certainty what the Globe in 1599 looked like or how much the one of today resembles it. Despite all the research that went into the project, some mysteries remain unsolved. As

Hildy says, however, "the discipline lies in the attempt, not in achieving rightness."[7]

Reconstructing the Globe in London required compromises. For example, the roof: although it is the first thatched roof in London since the great fire in 1666, builders had to install a sprinkler system for safety regulations. After a long debate about the Globe's size—there were scholars, like Hildy, who argued for a smaller Globe consisting of eighteen instead of the twenty bays—they were unable to solve the problem, and a vote was taken. Finally, the Globe was built as a twenty-sided polygonal.

There are also compromises concerning the use of the stage today. Rehearsals take place in rehearsal rooms, the female parts are not played by teenaged boys, and the texts that are used are often modern editions performed with today's pronunciation. As for the surroundings of the Globe: the foyer, the cafe, and the souvenir shop are all features of a modern theatre business.

Despite all the critique, past seasons have shown that the question of authenticity is not really important when it comes to the acting onstage. It is the concept of the room, the ability to interact with a standing audience in daylight, that makes the acting on the Globe stage different from the experiences in typical theatres.

For the artistic director Mark Rylance authenticity therefore means "nothing unless it's authenticity that reveals better methods of doing things, that helps the plays function and work in new and unexpected ways."[8] Still, in several past productions Rylance has shown an interest in producing Shakespeare in originally reconstructed costumes but, as he says, only "as long as they are linked or trying to link with a strong intention to communicate more than just their own form for form's sake."[9]

Costume designer Jenny Tiramani explains: "We want the actors to wear realistic 16th-century clothes, in order to experience the effects these have on the movements and behaviour and this informs us about the reality of Elizabethan theatre."[10] The same applies to the use of reconstructed instruments that should help to judge the Globe's acoustics. Both features are not there to enhance the criticized antiquated atmosphere but are subjects of research.

In the productions of *Henry V* in 1997, *Antony and Cleopatra* in 1999, and *Twelfth Night* in 2002 the Globe introduced authentic costumes and experimented with the use of Tudor conventions like all-male casts. In the 2003 season, for the first time, there was a Women's Company performing *Richard III* and *The Taming of the Shrew*. Rylance explains: "Shakespeare's original actors were not limited by the gender of the parts they played, but enjoyed a revolutionary theatre of the imagination where commoner played king, man played woman, and, within the plays, woman man. . . . It is the presence of [the audience's] intelligent, humorous, and generous imagination in the Globe which inspires [the Globe's] creation."[11]

Rylance insists that the Globe is not a museum but that it is used as a laboratory that can help us to rediscover Shakespeare and present his plays in a new way. He says: "It would be sad if [the Globe] became a purist house. I'm all for people trying what they want on that stage, as long as they realize it's a new kind of stage. If they want to interpret, they'll have to figure out new ways of interpreting. There is absolutely no point in building sets, they must do it minimally."[12]

As I have mentioned, the London Globe is an invention, an ideal Elizabethan theatre based on research, as well as on a lot of guesswork. It combines all the information that we have today and proves that theory works in practice. Because the Globe has been rebuilt as authentically as possible, there is the chance that its architecture will teach us something about Shakespeare's original acting style. This can be seen as an innovation for performing the plays that are four hundred years old. Andrew Gurr explains: "The plays might be seen as a form of software, designed to fit a particular machine or piece of hardware, and we need to reconstruct the hardware the plays were designed for so that we can see more clearly how these supremely rich and intricate programs were designed to work."[13]

The innovation lies in the meeting of two different systems. Acting at the Globe can certainly help us to get more insights into Shakespeare's dramaturgy and the way the stage can be used effectively. But whatever the results are, they will be received and judged by a modern audience. The actors facing the challenges of the stage are actors of today, and their approaches are based on techniques of today. In that respect working at the Globe might not be authentic, as the actors are not pretending to be Elizabethan actors that are performing for an Elizabethan audience.

Since the Globe opened as a theatre in 1997 sixteen of Shakespeare's plays, six of his contemporaries' plays, and two new plays commissioned for the Globe have been produced on its stage. It is the Globe's policy that every year the company consists of at least six actors that have played the stage before. That way one tries to pass on knowledge and to compensate for the fact that there is not an ensemble that can build its work on the experiences made in previous productions.

The Globe's theatre season is complemented by an education season that runs year-round. Actors and practitioners offer a variety of programs developed for schools and university students, and a series of staged readings called "Read not Dead" also contributes to the exploration of non-Shakespearean repertoires. Education director Patrick Spottiswoode explains: "Globe education keeps the heart pumping and the blood running through the galleries of the Globe year round. It has helped to give visibility and credibility."[14]

After years of scholarly research about the building and its architecture, it is now the practitioner's task to find new insights into the dramaturgy of Shakespeare's plays by experimenting with the use of the stage and observing the audience's perception. In recent years some interesting discoveries have been made, especially concerning staging and blocking of plays, as well as the use of props, furniture, and costumes. In the following I will offer a few examples in which the fusion of playhouse architecture, language, action, and audience is impressively revealed.

In the Globe the audience embraces the stage on three sides and during daylight—and even when performances are held at night, daylight is imitated by a lighting system. At all times audience and actors are in full view of each other. This is not only one of the most striking differences from contemporary theatres, but it means that there is a completely different viewing experience for the audience.

Today it seems unimaginable that in the twenty-five hundred years of theatre history the auditorium was darkened only about a hundred years ago. Since then the audience has become an anonymous passive mass of voyeurs that are sitting behind the so-called fourth wall, which separates the auditorium from the stage. At the Globe there is no fourth wall; actors and audience share the same room and light.

Before the actors step onto the Globe's stage for the first time, they are often terrified. It is not only the vastness of the empty stage that can be intimidating, but to see seventeen hundred people in the galleries and yard and to be seen by them in broad daylight can be extremely frightening. Actors soon realize, however, that it is not scary at all. The experience they all talk about is that of a huge embrace. The actress Anastasia Hille explains:

> The circular shape and the height of the house creates a cyclic energy that goes round and intensifies. Sitting in the house is just as exciting as being on the stage, because of the different focus and sensations in different areas of the theatre. The stage juts into the audience, so that at certain points you have these incredible perspectives. The "all the world is a stage" metaphor will perhaps recapture their potency in this capsule of cosmology. There is a mixture of being enclosed and open at the same time—you feel

embraced and very safe, but you feel the huge possibilities of chaos too. I think it's going to draw tremendous performances out of people.[15]

Watching or listening to a play in Shakespeare's time was a totally different event than it is today. Going to the theatre today is a well-planned event. We usually book tickets in advance and read the reviews before we decide what we are going to see. We dress up, meet in the foyers with a glass of champagne, and then sit passively in the darkened auditorium, watching the director's concept and interpretation of a play. It may appear that directors and actors do not even care about the audience.

The director Eimuntas Nekrosius, for example, says:

> I am not interested whether the audience likes the performance or not. If they are leaving the room then the room is empty and it does not matter. I am there and the stage is there. Art is only an expression of oneself. It's only serving one's own pleasure and satisfaction. The opinion that art has to serve the people, it has to be moral and delight is not true at all. Each artist is only speaking about oneself.[16]

Director and actor Mark Rylance says something very different about the Globe: "Shakespeare gives us plays, and an acoustic theatre space in which to hear language together. Our modern technical world has benefits, but those benefits are often linked with increased isolation, in our cars, by our computers, in our minds. The Globe is a social place where light, sound, emotions and thoughts are shared by actor and audience alike."[17]

Going to the Globe today does not mean to have a comfortable chair where you can doze off when you feel bored. Here you either stand as a groundling in front of the stage, or you get a seat on one of the wooden benches in the galleries around the stage. It's only in the gentlemen's boxes that you can sit on a cushioned chair. Standing in front of the stage—where usually the best and most expensive seats are placed in common theatres—is by far the most interesting and unique experience. It distinguishes performances at the London Globe from all other theatre venues, as no other Globe replica offers the audience any standing room around the stage.

Having no comfort is one way to realize the whole time that we are physically there. The exhausting pain of standing three hours can be resisted by moving around and getting involved while enjoying the chance of changing perspectives on what is happening onstage. Still, it will take a few years before people in the audience will no longer insist on keeping their standing spot even after the interval or will not ask you to be silent during the performance. The more lively an audience the more challenging is the acting onstage, as the actors have to work hard to get back the people's attention. This is when the interaction begins and the audience becomes a partner to the actors.

Past seasons at the Globe have shown that it is the standing audiences in front of the stage that are the steering wheel of a performance. They can sway the mood of the whole theatre as they carry the energy of the stage to the people sitting further away and above. The same happens when the action is taken down into the yard. Theatre historians remain uncertain of the extent to which the actors of Shakespeare's time used the yard as an extension of the stage.

In several productions the actors of the new Globe used the yard very effectively, for example for entrances and exits. It was used most strikingly in *The Tempest*, when Ariel, released by Prospero, left the stage by wandering through the audience, admiring the "brave new world" that was embracing him. In the *As You Like It* production in 1998 the wrestling between Orlando and Charles took place among the groundlings, and in *Julius Caesar* (1999) actors were standing in the yard among the crowd. By representing the "Friends, Romans, countrymen" that are addressed by Brutus, these actors were establishing a vigorous relationship between stage and audience. Who could have predicted with what power a standing crowd can shape and influence the action onstage?

We now know the presence of a standing audience has released a sense of energy, mobility, and involvement that is missing in any other theatre. There is the potential that plays performed at the Globe reveal another level of understanding. One of the most interesting experiences in that respect was the production of *The Merchant of Venice*, where the part of Shylock was played by the German actor Norbert Kentrup.

The perception of the performances at the Globe was a unique one, as for the first time there was the opportunity for an audience to react to the action onstage and to reveal the sympathy or dislike for the Jew spontaneously under the Globe's open roof. Still, every performance was different, and Kentrup says that each day there was an uncertainty about how the audience would react. In one of the performances, for example, there was a lady sitting in the gentlemen's box who was constantly shouting, "Usurer," when Kentrup entered the stage. This encouraged the rest of the audience, especially the groundlings, to join in the hissing and shouting.

Kentrup, who had first ignored the reaction, addressed his speech in act 3, scene 1 not only directly to his enemies onstage, Salerio and Solanio, but to the lady's followers in the yard: "The villainy you teach me I will execute, and I shall go hard but will better the instruction." A few scenes later the lady, now drinking champagne and eating the food that was served to her by a black man in a white jacket, shouted again, "Usurer"; this time Kentrup addressed his following lines directly to her, while the audience again was completely quiet and listened carefully, observing the lady:

> What judgement shall I dread doing no wrong?
> You have among you many a purchas'd slave,
> Which like your asses, and your dogs and mules,
> You use in abject and in slavish parts,
> Because you bought them. (4.1.89–93)

At the end of the speech Kentrup asked the audience looking around: "I stand for judgement,—answer shall I have it?" The audience answered with applause and with this reaction showed that the Jew had convinced them and at that moment got their sympathy.

This is just one example showing that the actor has to be constantly aware of the audience and that the way he articulates and addresses his text gives him power to manipulate the audience's reactions and create sympathy for a character. Kentrup explains: "When you realize what it is like when hundreds of people in the Globe hate and mock you, then you develop a kind of hate yourself and all you want is revenge. Playing Shylock at the Globe made me suddenly aware from where he gets his motivation to react as he does in act 4, when he demands revenge."[18]

The example shows that Shakespeare must have expected the audience's provocative reactions and therefore built the actor's reaction into his dramaturgy. Playing *The Merchant of Venice* at the Globe shows that the reactions today do not differ and that the text still fits the audience's response. Since the opening of the Globe thousands of playgoers have been confronted with these new experiences. Nobody would have expected the audience's participation in the experiment of rebuilding the Globe because in former attempts at copying Shakespeare's theatre the audience did not really play an important part. They were mainly seen as tourists coming to be entertained.

We realize, besides all the scholarly work on text and dramaturgy in combination with the building, that it is the audience that should now become the focus of our research. The productions at the Globe clearly show that the audience, whether it consists of tourists or theatregoers, is the touchstone of success. It is the playhouse's architecture that supports a direct and active engagement between actors and audience, and the play texts written for these Elizabethan playhouses are full of devices that enhance that engagement.

Just like the actors are learning over the years how to use the Globe's space and stage, the audience will learn how to react and interact with the actors. It is a natural improvement that takes place. It has to do with the fact that despite the assumption that the audience only consists of tourists, there are audiences that will come back and rely on their experiences from the past.

As we have seen, despite some of the critics' opinions that the historical reconstruction of the Globe is "essentially kitsch—and part of the heritage industry,"[19] there is a potential that the new Globe can be seen as a tool for getting a better understanding of Shakespeare's dramaturgy and the effect it has on actors and audiences today.

It took nearly four hundred years to rebuild Shakespeare's Globe. After restoring the original texts Tieck and Poel built stages to suit the dramaturgy. With the restoring of the original look of the theatre Thomas Wood Stevens attracted the tourists. These became an audience by watching the plays at the festival theatres that were featuring the essential elements of the Elizabethan playhouses. With the more or less authentic reconstruction of the Globe building in London, text and audience come together in a unique ensemble as for the first time all three elements—architecture, actors, and audience—are playing equal parts.

The use of the London Globe in the next years will show what function it will serve in the future. Critics of the Globe should not get irritated by the historical looks of the Globe and its stage, as the excitement lies in the modern context. It is the fact that it is an old building in a modern context that makes the Globe valuable. As a piece of art the building will definitely stay a tourist attraction, but its theatrical value is that it is an exciting venue in which to bring audiences together—audiences that consist of tourists as well as theatre people and scholars. With the potential of being a theatre as well as a place of research, the Globe can offer a close and unique union between practitioners and the academic world. If both parties stay open-minded, it could be "a tempestuous marriage with no possibility of divorce,"[20] as Rylance says.

Most fascinating about all the global reconstructions is the fact that a development can be observed. Since the rebuilding of the Globe in London there have been several attempts to build a Globe as an innovative theatre. Architects of Globe replicas in Japan, Switzerland, the Czech Republic, and Germany tried to preserve the essential elements of the Globe architecture without being historically or authentically correct. Built with materials and technical skills of today, all these theatres consist of a thrust stage surrounded by three ranges of galleries for the audience and a tiring house with doors and balconies. Most of them even have an open roof. However, in size they resemble more the original Rose than the Globe, as most of them only measure between twenty-one and twenty-three meters in diameter.

One early example is the Globe in Neuss, Germany, which was opened in 1991. Originally built in 1988 for an amateur theatre group in Rheda Wiedenbrueck, today it houses a very successful annual International Shakespeare Festival. Built from wood and steel and measuring twenty-one meters in diameter, it is the smallest of all Globe replicas. Here, no one in the audience sits further away from the stage than ten meters.

In Tokyo, Japan, a replica of Shakespeare's Globe was designed by the famous Japanese architect Arata Isozaki. Based on data of Hollar's etching, de Witt's Swan drawing, and the Fortune contract, the concrete Globe was designed as a modern version of the Globe and equipped with the latest stage mechanisms. It was opened in 1988 and never housed its own company. International directors and touring groups were invited, including the London Globe's company, which brought two of its productions there. Unfortunately, because of financial problems the so-called Panasonic Globe had to be closed in 2002, and its future remains uncertain.

A charming little Globe replica was built in Lichtensteig in Switzerland in 1998. Here it was a young theatre producer who had the idea to copy the Globe as an homage to the Swiss poet Ulrich Bräker, whose bicentennial death day was celebrated in 1998. Bräker's admiration of Shakespeare's work had inspired him to write his drama *The Judgement-night, or What You Will*—a play that was never performed in his lifetime. While looking for a suitable venue in which to produce this play, producer Lukas Levenberger had the idea to build a Globe replica. Built with the help of modern technology, this twelve-sided Globe consisted of 270 wooden pieces. Just like in Shakespeare's time, the wooden skeleton was prefabricated off-site then joined together on-site like a jigsaw puzzle in less than two weeks.

The designer's main aim was not to rebuild a historical theatre but to recreate the atmosphere of the Globe's room concept; therefore, no historical material was consulted. Still, the result was a fascinating little "wooden O." After a successful summer, with thirty performances of Bräker's play, the Globe was dismantled and offered to be sold. Eventually, the Europa-Park in Rust, near Freiburg, in the south of Germany, bought it and turned it into a nostalgic-looking Globe, which is no longer used as a theatre but serves as a tourist attraction in the "English Corner" of the famous German fun park.

Another "wooden O" was erected in Prague, Czech Republic, in 1999. Built in a very simple way, with plain wood, it measures thirty meters in diameter, just like the Globe in Tokyo and the one in London. Concentrating on the main elements of the Elizabethan theatre, builders renounced any decoration and the facade consists of wooden panels that are transparent. Apart from a short season each summer, where a local theatre company plays Shakespeare, some touring companies present their plays. Unfortunately, at the moment the so-called Globe '99 is fighting for its existence.

The latest Globe is the "Ice Globe" in North Sweden. The building was constructed from snow, faced, where appropriate, with gravestone-sized rectangles of clear ice, roughly fifteen centimeters deep. It was built in three weeks, opened in January 2003, and melted away at the beginning of April. Having been inspired by the London Globe, it was a fascinating piece of art, an "icy O," offering ninety-six seats in the boxes of the one-story gallery and standing space in the yard for 424 groundlings, who could watch Hamlet at minus 35 degrees Celsius.

The latest full-scale wooden Globe replica was opened in the year 2000, again in southern Germany, in a small town called Schwaebisch Hall, which is known for its famous annual theatre festival. The town was looking for something new and exciting to celebrate the festival's seventy-fifth anniversary. After visiting the Bräker Globe in Switzerland, they decided to build one as well.

A team of six architects got together and planned a mobile sixteen-sided Globe with a diameter of twenty-three meters. Just like the one in Switzerland it consists of numerous prefabricated pieces and can be installed and dismantled in a very short time. Instead of a historic-looking facade or stage decoration, builders decided to keep the Globe transparent and invented an innovative solution for the stair turrets: only every second one leads up to the top gallery. What impresses most is the aesthetic purity of the wooden room, combined with modern materials like steel and glass. Here, the idea of the Elizabethan theatre has found a modern interpretation.

Although it will take a while for directors and actors to learn how to use the stages effectively, there have already been some remarkable ideas of interpreting the new old space. What can be generally observed is, again, the great influence the audience has on the performances.

This therefore proves it is the room concept of the Globe that enhances new ways of performing and perceiving Shakespeare's plays today. A theatre type that was invented four hundred years ago becomes an innovative playhouse today. And the new Globes demonstrate that the development of the Elizabethan theatre that had come to an end by the closure of the playhouses in 1642 can now continue. It will be fascinating to watch where this realization will lead. As the Chorus says in the prologue to act 2 of Shakespeare's *Henry V*: "For now sits expectation in the air . . . "

Notes

1. Ekkehart Krippendorf, "This 'Wooden O,'" *Freitag*, Aug. 29, 1997 (translated into English by the author).

2. John Drakakis, "Dr. Strangelove: or How I Learned to Trust in the Globe and Set Fire to My Dreams," *European English Messenger* 4, no. 1 (1995): 16.

3. For details see Franklin J. Hildy's essay in this volume.

4. Quoted from an undated letter from Allardyce Nicoll to Marjorie Morris found by the author in the archive of The Globe of the Great Southwest.

5. C. Walter Hodges, "What Is Possible: The Art and Science of Mistakes," in *New Issues in the Reconstruction of Shakespeare's Theatre*, ed. F. J. Hildy (New York: P. Lang, 1990), 47, 52.

6. Franklin J. Hildy, "Why Authenticity," lecture delivered at the International Globe Conference "Shakespeare and Tudor Theatrical Traditions," Sep. 11, 1996, London.

7. Ibid.

8. Quoted in Barry Day, *This Wooden 'O': Shakespeare's Globe Reborn* (London: Oberon Books, 1996), 279.

9. Mark Rylance, "A Vision Fair and Fortunate" (interview by Nicholas Robins), *The Globe* (winter 1995/96): 4.

10. Jenny Tiramani, *Henry V* playbill (1997).

11. London Globe season's brochure 2003, 2.

12. Quoted in Day, *This Wooden 'O'*, 279.

13. Andrew Gurr, "Rebuilding the Globe with the Arts of Compromise," *Shakespeare Jahrbuch* (1990): 11.

14. Patrick Spottiswoode, e-mail to the author, July 10, 2002.

15. Anastasia Hille, quoted in Vanessa Schormann, *Shakespeare's Globe, Rekonstruktionen, Repliken, und Bespielbarkeit* (Heidelberg: C. Winter, 2002), 346.

16. Eimuntas Nekrosius, "Ein System Habe Ich Nicht," (interview with B. Lehmann), in *Die Deutsche Buehne. Das Theatermagazin* 8 (1996): 17 (translated by the author).

17. Mark Rylance, quoted in the London Globe season's brochure, 1999, 1.

18. Norbert Kentrup, quoted in Schormann, *Shakespeare's Globe*, 338.

19. W. B. Worthen, "Reconstructing the Globe: Constructing Ourselves," *Shakespeare Survey* 52 (1999): 35.

20. Quoted in Day, *This Wooden 'O'*, 279.

Symposium Response

A T THE END OF THE weekend Drs. Hildy and Schormann shared their impressions of the conference and their thoughts on the most important themes that were explored. What follows are excerpts from that conversation, with some minor clarifications of thought.

FRANKLIN J. HILDY [FJH]: We'll start out with Vanessa, talking about what she's picked up.

VANESSA SCHORMANN [VS]: I'll just throw in a few of the issues we've covered. I've divided it into the main issues I thought we touched on—space and theatre, audience, authenticity, and adapting. What I'll do now is just mention some of my notes; Frank and I will just have a few words about it and then open it up to you for discussion.

So, concerning "space and theatre," I wrote down theatre archetypes, tourist venues, modified space, inside and outside, as well as scenery. In my view, all that leads us back to the question, why do we rebuild Shakespeare's theatre, and if we do it, in what way do we rebuild it?

For "audiences" I wrote down expectation, attracting an audience, . . . changing it, meeting the audience, taking them seriously, as well as looking at the audience's role in general, and stirring the audience's imagination . . . which leads up to the question, for whom are we producing Shakespeare?

And then the issue of "authenticity"—which leads up to the question, do we need authenticity? And also looking at the issue of adapting Shakespeare, something that has been done regularly since the nineteenth century, what does it involve? I wrote down "adding to the play, bending the text, translating, transmission, concept Shakespeare, popular culture, references to our time." All this is leading to the question, what do we gain by adapting or bending the text?

So—to wrap it up, we focused on issues concerning the actor/audience relationship and authenticity, as well as the aesthetics of Shakespeare's theatre and his plays in the past and today.

FJH: And that is a ton of stuff to come out of a conference. I was thinking about this session last night and how I might approach it. The topic was "Elizabethan Performance in North American Spaces," and it occurred to me that because of my bias and Vanessa's bias toward exploring the relationship between Elizabethan performances and spaces, we've tended to focus a lot on spaces that have been designed specifically for Elizabethan performances. But of course 99.9 percent of all productions of Elizabethan plays done in North America are done in other kinds of spaces that have nothing whatsoever [to] do with the Elizabethans or our attempt to recreate Elizabethan spaces. And I think the papers today [the Sunday of the conference] reflect working with these plays in totally different spaces. Working in a proscenium arch, working in that abandoned factory setting, which is a beautiful setting for *Hamlet*, isn't it? I guess a number of things really struck me yesterday and the day before and this morning—when you listen to all these papers where people are trying to solve problems in all these different ways, it reminds me of just how incredibly versatile theatre people have always been. And then if you compare it to the present, it's the same thing— people trying to solve problems in a very versatile way. But I was trying to think of what the problem is that people have been trying to solve with all this versatility. I am not sure I know how to articulate this.

And it has occurred to me on many occasions that, when people enter the theatre as a profession, they can decide to just do it, and just do whatever work comes their way, and take theatre as they found it. But a lot of people come into theatre and they want to make it better than they found it, so they want to make it the best theatre they can possibly make it, and that depicts a slightly different way of approaching theatre. Then I guess another way people come to theatre is they really don't like the theatre that they come into and they want to change it. They have a different vision of what theatre ought to be, and they want to change theatre to match that vision.

So if we look at people in the nineteenth century, most are just doing theatre as they found it, but then you've got people like Henry Irving and [Herbert Beerbohm] Tree trying to make Shakespearean productions the best that they could possibly be, given the theatre that they had to work with. And then you have people like William Poel, coming along and saying, "You know, this is wrong; this is not the way we ought to be doing theatre." And of course Poel was part of a much bigger group (that included the Crafts movement in England), with all those antirealist experiments; they were all moving in the same direction, saying, "You know what? The kind of thing that Tree and Irving have been doing is the wrong way for people to go, and so we want to change that." And it's harder to see in our own time the people who are trying to make major changes in the way theatre is done, but obviously there are people doing that. Robert Wilson's work is essentially saying, "Theatre has been going [in] the wrong direction; we need to go [in] a totally different direction in theatre." And so it's really intriguing to see that in some ways theatre hasn't changed much.

You have to think that people in Shakespeare's day were just as versatile. You must have had the majority of theatre people in that period saying, "I like theatre, and I just want to take it as it is. As long as I can do it, I'm happy, and I don't have any strong feelings that it needs to change or it needs to be something different. I like what I'm doing, and I want to keep doing it." You must also have had people who were trying to make theatre the best theatre they could make it, given the tools they thought theatre ought to be making use of; and you must have had people saying, "We're just going the wrong way; we've got to do something different here." I wonder which group Shakespeare belonged to? And thinking in those terms, again, it just seems like there's such fascinating stuff going on. And what accounts for that? And what do people work with, when they start saying either "I want to perfect theatre" or "I want to change theatre"?

Another issue that came up for me over the last few days has to do with the audience expectations Vanessa talked about. You know, because of my interest in architecture I tend to think about audiences in terms of the space they enter, but so much of what we are all concerned with does lead back to expectation—what is the audience expectation when they attend a performance? The production for me starts as soon as the first piece of publicity goes out. As soon as *The Falstaff Project* title went out—that started to set the audience's expectations. But now I'm wondering, in terms of Shakespeare, isn't it an even bigger thing? Because there's an entire Shakespeare culture at work out there. For the major plays—many people haven't read them, but they still think they know them. So they know *Hamlet*, but they've never actually read it. And then of course there are huge numbers of people who have read it. In the nineteenth century it seems like an awful lot of people read Shakespeare. You read these stories of early explorers of the American continent. In their canoes they would have the Bible, and they would have Shakespeare. But that means that whenever you take on a Shakespeare play you have a whole different set of problems because the whole idea of expectation is much broader now than what you face with any other playwright, and certainly any other Elizabethan playwright, since the topic is Elizabethan performances. How can you ever meet the expectations an audience has for a Shakespeare production? It's much easier to do things with Middleton, Beaumont, and Fletcher, any of those other people, than it is when you try to deal with Shakespeare, because most people don't have any expectations for their plays. I think in the nineteenth century they tried to surpass audience expectation by making the plays grander, more beautiful, more impressive than anyone could have expected. That is very hard to do given the vividness of the language. Today I'm not sure we even try. It is much easier to imagine the audience as having rather low expectations and then just subverting those. The problem is you must always look for new ways to subvert, and you feel obligated to out-subvert the last subversion, and that can lead to a lot of silly rationalizations.

Earlier in the conference we were talking about the adaptations of Shakespeare, and that seems somehow linked to all this. People adapt the plays to subvert expectations so they can make some new and insightful modern point. But I was wondering—if you're going to adapt the story, why bother to include chunks of Shakespeare's play when you do that? Why don't we just do what Shakespeare did and take a popular story and refashion [it in] whatever way we like to make whatever point we like? The recent film *Ten Things I Hate about You* I think did just that. This [approach] eliminates the problem of dealing with iambic pentameter and verse and having to call guns swords and all of that. But obviously we rarely do that in modern theatre because we know that if you put Shakespeare's name on a production, more people will feel like they need to go see it. And if you just put your name on it, they may or may not decide to go see it. So we are trading on Shakespeare's reputation, and we're using Shakespeare's reputation to legitimize what we're doing, in a way that it would not be legitimized if we simply put our own names on it. And that's an intriguing cultural issue that everyone has to negotiate, in one way or another. If we are going to trade on an artist's reputation, what do we owe to the work that gave that artist that reputation? And it seems to me that what we've been looking at for the last couple of days is the way people have negotiated that problem. And again, I've been very focused on Elizabethan revival, which is one way of negotiating that issue, but obviously all of the postmodern approaches that you see used are a totally different way of dealing with that problem.

Getting back to expectations, you can meet expectations, you can exceed expectations, or you can subvert expectations. I think a lot of modern theory focuses on the subversion of expectations in production, and certainly that's true in a lot of modern Shakespeare productions, where they intentionally undermine the text, or deconstruct the text; they intentionally reorganize it; they do a lot of things so that you know as soon as they start performing that you've got to throw all your expectations out the window and just hope to God they come up with something neat by the end because otherwise you're going to be really bored. But that's really the context I would put it in, is this notion of expectation and then what people think about the theatre world that they inherited.

One of the reasons that I'm so fixated on theatre history is because when we enter the theatre we haven't entered into a vacuum. We do what we do in response to what the last generation did. And we might respond to that last generation by saying, "Boy, those people really sucked, and I could do so much better than they did." When you look at the history of what people say about acting, you have almost a consistent pattern of critics saying, "You know that last generation of actors just chewed the scenery and were just terrible overactors, but if you want to see acting that's like real life, that really holds the mirror up to nature, our modern actors do that." And then twenty-five years later they're saying, "That last generation of actors just ate the scenery; they were so phony and unrealistic, and it's our actors that really hold the mirror up to nature." It's a weird repeating phenomenon.

vs: What comes to my mind, concerning the question about Shakespeare's reputation, is the question, why do we ask that? Why does Shakespeare have that reputation? Why do we do all that to his plays? And I think it goes back to the fact that Shakespeare was writing for an audience, he was writing for a specific theatre, and he was writing in such an open way that we can do all these things, today and for all these centuries.

fjh: The thing that always intrigues me about that is that Jonson was writing for that kind of theatre, Middleton was writing for that kind of theatre, and I think Middleton was one of the most underrated playwrights in that period. I think in many ways he was a more versatile playwright than Shakespeare, and a lot of his stuff was really brilliant, and I'm looking forward to more people doing those plays, but I hope they will trust the text. I was very disappointed in the first two seasons at the Globe; they did Middleton plays, which was great, but they clearly had no faith in the production, in the text. They really felt like they had to jazz up the text, and they had to have all kinds of things [on the stage], and my preference would have been to say, "Hey, just do the text for me and let me see if I like it or not." And then play with it after that, but give [it] a chance, because I'm in the Globe; I'd like to see you trust the text. Now if I had seen it in this room, then I don't care what you do with it that much, as long as you find some way of dealing with the fact that the language is very very different from what people speak, and if you can make the visuals and the language match up in some way, I don't care what way you do that, just so there's some kind of attempt and some kind of realization that there's a language here that has to be recognized as special in some way.

And why haven't the plays of the other playwrights from the period been done more? *A New Way to Pay Old Debts* was produced much more often than Shakespeare's plays for the two hundred years after the Restoration; why don't we have a revival of a play that would be as successful as that one was? And what is it that has made Shakespeare so successful? . . . I think there is a reason *Hamlet*'s done, and has been done for so long; I think there is a reason why Shakespeare's plays are done more often: because ultimately I think that they have been found to be better plays. People consider them to be better and more interesting to listen to. The Globe has been a driving force behind that move to do other plays by other playwrights. So when the Swan opened, that was one of the things they started out with, was to look at a lot of these other playwrights. . . . But this new original-practices movement (it was called the Elizabethan Revival a hundred years ago) is, I think, behind that interest in a lot of these other Elizabethan plays. How long that movement is going to last I don't know. I know that the great outcome of the Elizabethan Revival was the proliferation of thrust stages; it really gave a legitimacy to the whole thrust-stage idea, and theatres all over the world felt like they had to have at least one thrust stage available to them after that movement. My prediction would be that the great legacy of this original-practices movement that we're involved in now will be the recognition of the value of a standing audience. Not that all your audience has to stand, in fact you wouldn't want all your audience to stand, but a standing audience with a stacked auditorium—I think you're going to see a lot of adaptations of that.

[A discussion with the audience of youth culture and their reaction to Elizabethan theatre and producing theatre followed, and then Dr. Schormann brought the discussion back on topic by talking about the value of the architectural research being done, which may help some young people connect with Elizabethan theatre. Dr. Hildy then discussed the similarities with what people went through in the nineteenth century.

They, too, debated the value of researching the original theatrical form because the audiences were so different that they could never really understand the plays in the same way. He ended with a question:]

FJH: Is the difference between an Elizabethan audience and a modern audience so great that we really can't bridge that gap? And if it is that great, then how come the plays are still interesting to us?

AUDIENCE MEMBER [AM]: Something that just crossed my mind is that in my observations of art . . . and language, I see more facility with the young amateurs now than there was twenty years ago—and I think it's because we've had twenty years of rap music. That we are used to rhythm in speech and—it used to be that you would just sort of grit your teeth for Shakespeare because it was just so appalling, and now I'm not even aware of the language because it is facilitated by a different mode of speech that we are all attuned to. I think this may be one of the reasons that we are again attracted to Shakespeare, and it's a much more pop-culture thing. The other thing that I want to throw out is this idea—there are so many more access points than we've had before, because our ears have changed, because people want to be involved, and theatre is seen less as going into the traditional proscenium theatre, where people of only culture and wealth are able to participate. Theatre has changed.

VS: I want to go back to when you said we're more attuned to the language and rhythm today. The question is, then why are there so many textual and visual add-ons to the plays, as well as all these projections, etc.? As soon as you have all these technical things coming up as well, you can't concentrate on the language.

AM: But do you have to concentrate on the language? The language is just what you hear. You don't have to go, "Oh my goodness, this is the most beautiful poetic language." The language just simply conveys the characters, the ideas, the conflicts, the emotions. We're no longer having to focus on the language because it just enters into us.

VS: But [if it's all in the text], and if you don't understand that because you just flow on that rhythm, then you have to visualize again what it says in the text; otherwise it's going to get [confused].

FJH: Well, if you think about rap music[ians] . . . they establish a beat, and then they force the words into the beat. There's no sense of meter there; they just sort of force it in, and you can put as many syllables as

you want, as long as you keep that beat driving behind you. And some
people are better than others at it. The most interesting thing to do is
to see rap music written out, all the lyrics are available on the Web. Take
a look at the way they're written out, and you'll see that there isn't any
meter really; it's just the way they say it, the way they deliver it, can
force it into that constant beat. And it works very effectively, but it's a
very different form from what teachers like Patrick Tucker and Neil
Freeman talk about in their studies of Shakespeare's verse in performance. Neil talks about it being like your own heartbeat, and he's been
looking at what happens when that heartbeat changes. What happens
when you put an extra foot on a line or an extra two feet on a line?
What happens when you break that heartbeat? What happens when one
person finishes in the middle of a line and the other person picks up
the middle of the line? What happens when the heartbeat stops and you
go into prose? That's a very very different thing than what happens in
rap music, it seems to me. Which is not to say that rap music hasn't
given us more sensitivity.

   Actually, I would say that people like Neil, the work they are doing
in going back to the text and really trying to look at what's going on
with the text, have been very influential in this process. Patrick Tucker
in England has worked along similar lines. . . . There was a real fashion
at the Royal Shakespeare Company and mostly at Royal Academy of
Dramatic Art a few years back when they were working really to train
actors how to deliver Shakespeare lines as if they weren't poetry or verse.
Actors had to work really hard to make the lines "gritty" and "real"
and like "real language" so that you could hide the fact that this was
poetry. And then they went to a phase where what they really wanted
to do was deliver the lines and put breaks at weird places or put emphasis
at weird places, because the idea was that that forces the audience to
think. You've subverted their expectation, and so they have to think
about the line now, in weird ways. And also, it makes you distinctive as
an actor. You're not doing what everybody else does; you now have a
distinctive trait as an actor, and that will get you cast more often.
There's nothing wrong with that. Those are perfectly legitimate things
to do, and I would argue that once Barry Jackson got us all committed
to doing modern-dress productions, after his 1921 or 1922 *Hamlet*, that
they had to start working to hide the fact that you were speaking verse,
because that was the only way to keep the visuals and the orals working
together. So it was fine to dress in 1920s costumes, as long as you hid
the fact that you were speaking verse. But if you emphasized the fact
that you were speaking verse, if you stressed the poetry, then you had
a problem.

Though, you're right, I think that this generation is pretty much better at speaking verse, for a variety of reasons, and rap music may be one of them, and the work that Patrick Tucker and Neil Freeman and others have been doing may be another one . . . and that's why this whole issue of the visual and the oral is more important to me now than it was twenty years ago, because they are doing the verse, and what does that mean in terms of the costuming? I would argue that in the Baz Luhrmann film of *Romeo and Juliet,* a lot of people have criticized DiCaprio; they've said, "Well, he just can't handle verse." I say, you know, if you put him in the same costuming that they did the Zeffirelli film in, I think you'd say, "He's a damn good actor." I think the problem is partly the environment he was put in, although given the choice that they made to update it, I think they made really brilliant choices in terms of the kind of costumes they selected. But I ran into the Zeffirelli film by accident on late-night television a few months ago, and they were doing the fight scene, and I thought, "Damn, they did a good job." I didn't watch the whole thing, so maybe I wouldn't have been impressed if I'd seen the whole thing, but that fight scene, whoa. And the language was so clear and sharp and really amazing. But that is because the visuals worked with the language, and that is not what happens when you put the plays in a modern setting but still try to retain the original language. There is a relationship between language and environment—certainly between language and costuming.

AM: I wanted to ask you—that idea of the unity of text and costume—I just want to ask you if that idea doesn't discount the possibility that a discord between text and production does not actually heighten the text even more.

FJH: Everybody talks about it in terms of subverting the text . . .

AM: We talk about the costume being a barrier between the text and the audience; it gives the actor something to hide behind, and we take that all away . . .

FJH: And that is the standard approach; I can't think of a design meeting I've been in in the last twenty-five years where that isn't what they said—[this idea] of the contrast between the language and the design. And I always wondered why for me personally it didn't work. The idea is to eliminate the barrier, and for me you've created a barrier. At the Shakespeare Theatre Association of America we were talking about this two weeks ago, and the director from Atlanta Shakespeare, Jeff Watkins, said something like, "If it talks like a Duke, and it walks like a Duke, it's probably a Duke, so it ought to look like one." For him, using modern dress just added to the distance between him and the language. To change *Hamlet* into *The Godfather*, you're creating a disjuncture there. And if there's something intentionally you're doing with that, that's fine, but you ought to recognize what you're doing. And I'm just questioning that assumption that by neutralizing the costumes you're causing people to focus more on the verse. For me it creates a violation of my sense of what the eighteenth century would have referred to as verisimilitude, of truth-seemingness. And so I'm no longer willing to go with you on your voyage. Having said that, I must add that some of the most successful Shakespeare I've seen has been set in a kind of futuristic world, where they can bring a style to the costumes that matches the language, without feeling like there's some kind of discontinuity.

VS: But when you're talking about a production where you have a mixture of styles and times and materials . . . easily it becomes a sort of school-performance style, because there's nothing in between.

FJH: The thing is that we ought to always be arguing about it. I'd be frightened if I went to a theatre conference where everyone agreed.

[Discussion about productions that do simple, just-the-text versions of plays versus productions that liberally interpret the text]

AM: But particularly when we're talking about Shakespeare, we don't even know if that really is the text, right? We talk about the different texts of Shakespeare. We don't know how much it might have changed in performance from night to night, or how slavish they were to the words. To take it as a frozen artifact and say, "This is the text and therefore we're doing it the way Shakespeare intended" . . . we have no idea whether that's true.

FJH: And as you've heard over the course of these discussions, there's one group of people who say that what we need to do is to be true to the performance or true to the text and another group who says what you really need to do is to be true to the spirit of the text. And those can lead to very very different results, and they both have equally valid reasons for doing what they do. And my sense is that in any production that is done today that isn't an adaptation, they would say that they're being true to the text, or at least true to the spirit of the text. That does just mean that they're being true to the text as they understand it, but the point is they believe that there is a text to be true to, if only in spirit. And no matter how much the texts changed, the language was still very ornate. . . . But that doesn't address the issues that I'm interested in, right now. I'm really interested in what we can learn from the physical architecture of these theatre buildings that produced some remarkably successful dramatic literature, and some remarkably popular theatre, that seemed to have been popular not just for one small social class but was popular across classes in a way that has been rare in theatre. The only time we really see it again is in the late eighteenth, early nineteenth century. Even in Elizabethan times you didn't get very much audience from the lower classes; you don't get very much audience from the really upper classes (because if they wanted to see a play they just had you come to them; they didn't go to the playhouse). But you did have a huge cross-section of audience, a bigger cross-section of audience than you often see in theatre, and that fascinates me. I want to understand if the architecture had anything to do with that, and so far, from what we've seen at the Globe, it did. How much, and what we can do with that, I don't know.

Contributors

Aaron Anderson is assistant professor of Movement and Voice at Virginia Commonwealth University. He holds an MFA in Acting and Asian Theatre from the University of Hawai'i at Manoa and an interdisciplinary PhD in Theatre and Drama from Northwestern University. He is an internationally certified fight director and stage-combat instructor and has published widely on martial arts films, movement, and gender.

David Carlyon wrote *Dan Rice: The Most Famous Man You've Never Heard Of*, which was featured in the *New York Times* and the *New Yorker*. He was a clown with Ringling Brothers and Barnum & Bailey Circus for three years, a New York City actor during the 1980s, mostly in Shakespeare, and a professor at the University of Michigan-Flint, after receiving a PhD at Northwestern University. He has also been a military policeman, a forest-fire fighter, and a lawyer. Currently he is working on *Tartuffle-Dee, Tartuffle-Dum* (an adaptation of *Tartuffe*) and a script for *The Simpsons*.

Susan S. Cole is chair of the Department of Theatre and Dance at Appalachian State University. She is a past president of the Southeastern Theatre Conference and a contributor to *Notable Women in American Theatre* and other biographical works. She has published articles in *Southern Theatre* and other publications. Dr. Cole received her AB and MA from Stanford University and her PhD from the University of Oregon.

Sarah Ferguson, a Paetzold Fellow, moved to Vancouver to continue her work in the PhD program at the University of British Columbia after completing her MFA in directing at the University of Calgary. Presently, her work explores deconstruction of the traditional staging of canonical texts to uncover the cultural and social constructs embedded therein.

Richard L. Hay is the principal theatre and scenic designer of the Oregon Shakespeare Festival. Other theatre designs include the Old Globe Theatre in San Diego and two theatres for Denver Center Theatre. He has produced numerous other scenic designs across the country. Mr. Hay received his AB and MA from Stanford University.

Franklin J. Hildy received his PhD from Northwestern University and is professor of theatre history, former department chair, and head of the PhD program in Theatre and Performance Studies in the Department of Theatre at the University of Maryland. He is also director of The Shakespeare Globe Center (USA) Research Archive. Dr. Hildy has worked as a theatre consultant and has been an architectural adviser on the reconstruction of the 1599 Globe for the International Shakespeare Globe Center, London; for the reconstruction of the 1613 Globe for Shenandoah Shakespeare, Staunton, Virginia; and for the reconstruction of the 1587 Rose Theatre in Lenox, Massachusetts. He is the author of *Shakespeare at the Maddermarket: Nugent Monck and the Norwich Players* (1986), editor of *New Issues in the Reconstruction of Shakespeare's Theatre* (1990), and coauthor, with Oscar Brockett, of two editions of *History of the Theatre* (1999 and 2003). He has published a variety of articles on theatre space, Shakespearean staging techniques, the theatre architecture of the Spanish Golden Age, and baroque theatre.

Richard H. Palmer is professor of theatre at the College of William and Mary in Williamsburg, Virginia. He is author of *The Contemporary British History Play* (1998), *The Lighting Art* (2nd ed. 1994), *Tragedy and Tragic Theory* (1992), and *The Critics' Canon* (1988). A frequent contributor to periodicals, he is also associate editor of *Theatre Annual*. He is currently writing a book on technology and the playwright.

Johanna Schmitz earned her PhD from the University of California at Davis in 2001 with a dissertation titled "Desire for Authenticity: Millennial Reconstructions of Shakespeare's Theater," which focused on Shakespeare's Globe Theatre, the Rose exhibit, the set for *Shakespeare in Love*, and the proposed reconstruction of that set as a new theater. From 1997 to 2002 she was an instructor for the Shakespeare Globe Centre USA "Teaching Shakespeare through Performance" professional development course at Shakespeare's Globe in London. She is an assistant professor at Southern Illinois University, Edwardsville, where she teaches dramatic literature and performance theory and directs.

Vanessa Schormann is the author of *Shakespeare's Globe: Replicas, Reconstructions, and the Usage of the Stage* (Heidelberg: C. Winter, 2002). She is the executive director of the Shakespeare Globe Center–Germany and a board member of the German Shakespeare Society. She teaches in the Department of Drama at the Ludwig-Maximilians University, Munich, and is a freelance dramaturg for Shakespeare & Partner. Dr. Schormann holds a PhD from the Ludwig-Maximilians University in Munich.

Annie Smith is an actor, director, and theatre educator. She is currently a PhD student at the University of British Columbia. Her area of research is drama performance as a facilitating tool for community building. She is the past artistic director and is on the board of directors for Trickster's Theatre, a community-based aboriginal theatre company on Vancouver Island.

Kevin J. Wetmore Jr. is an assistant professor of theatre at California State University, Northridge, and the founding artistic director of the Unseam'd Shakespeare Company, an award-winning, Pittsburgh-based classical theatre company. He is the author of *The Athenian Sun in an African Sky: Modern African Adaptations of Classical Greek Tragedy* and *Black Dionysus: Greek Tragedy and African American Theatre*. He is also the editor of "Revenge: East and West" and coauthor of "Dude, Where's My Bard: Shakespeare and Youth Culture" (both works in progress).